Spirit on Fire

A Story of Love, Art & Healing

by
Jay Harden

Azalea Art Press
Sonoma | California

ISBN: 978-1-943471-45-4

Library of Congress Control Number: 2020915221

Cover Design
Created by Elizabeth Perlman | Oakland | California

Front Cover Photography
© Trotter Art | Creve Coeur | Missouri

Back Cover Photo
© Eric Mosvoid

for
Giggles

It is by going down into the abyss
that we recover the treasures of life.
Where you stumble,
there lies your treasure.

—*Joseph Campbell*

CONTENTS

Shona Harden | 2001

Foreword

The book you hold in your hands is a remembrance of one woman's courageous journey through life, but it is so much more—it is a love letter to the human spirit and our ability to rise above even the most heartbreaking challenges.

I prayed for Shona long before I knew her name. I often say that everything that is good about me is *because of Shona*. She was the first person to make my life make sense, the first to validate my perceptions and my worth, and the first to teach me how to love and trust myself.

A month before I met Shona, I stood alone on the Brooklyn Bridge, crying and praying for help. A few weeks later, just after my 25th birthday, I found myself at a design program in Atlanta when I heard the musical lilt of a British accent. I looked across the room and caught my breath—because there she was!

Shona had arrived at design school wearing a bright blue wig, glittering eye shadow and dozens of colorful bracelets, all clinking together joyfully. She was radiating light, as bright as the sun, and I loved her immediately. Right away, I wanted to spend every spare minute with her, to listen to her extraordinary stories and learn all the magical things she knew—because she knew *so many magical things*.

Imagine how you'd feel if Yoda, Obi-Wan Kenobi, Professor Dumbledore, Mary Poppins, Merlin, Glenda the Good Witch, and Cinderella's Fairy Godmother were combined into one person—and you just happened to be sitting next to them in a typography class. Sometimes I wonder if I was guided to design school just to meet Shona, the most magical person I have ever had the privilege of knowing.

Over the course our 19-year friendship and mentorship, Shona told me the story of her life, the story which has been so carefully researched and assembled here by her truly beautiful and heroic partner Jay Harden.

I spent countless hours at Shona and Jay's house when they were married, asking Shona questions about life, spirituality, and the nature of the universe. She always cooked incredible food and then we'd retreat to the Bedouin-style tent she had constructed for herself in the family room, a luxurious space lined with satin pillows, goddess sculptures, and her own sacred art. That was where she taught me about the wisdom of women and the power of the Divine Feminine.

Shona embodied the Divine Feminine in everything she did—the way she transformed paper into art, pain into healing, darkness into light. She was also shockingly skilled with cars. I'll never forget the time I went to visit her at her mountaintop home in North Georgia and my car stalled out, defeated by the steep, narrow curve of her driveway. I was in a panic, certain that my car was about to roll over the edge, but Shona made quick work of it, easing my car back into gear and ascending the almost-vertical incline with astounding speed and grace. In the prime of her life, Shona was as fearless as she was indomitable.

Through it all, Jay has loved Shona patiently, devotedly, and with all his heart. Although I have observed many relationships in my life, I have never met a man who has loved a woman as deeply, completely, and unconditionally as Jay loves Shona.

And yet, knowing what I know of Shona, it's only fitting. After all, Shona dedicated her life to healing her heart and reclaiming her power.

Shona taught me that the Divine Feminine is meant to be honored, treasured and cherished by the Divine Masculine, a truth Jay embodied every day he was with her. Jay offered Shona a depth of love that most of us are afraid to even hope for. Could a love like this actually exist, we wonder? I am here to say, *it does exist*, and Jay is the proof. Despite the intense pain that plagued her life, where Jay was concerned, I think Shona would say that she was indeed blessed.

Shona was without question a "Spirit on Fire." This book is a testament to one man's deep love for one extraordinary woman. May it inspire you as much as it has me.

— **Elizabeth Perlman**
Oakland, California
November 2020

Preface

The shortest distance between a human being and the truth is a story.

Shona's life was a tale of two stories: her inner story and her outer story. Her public story was one of great success across a range of incredible talents. She still is, to me, an almost mythical archetype of the warrior-goddess in search of self-knowledge and adventure. But the foundation of that is a repeated story of horrors and survival against great odds.

Shona lived life to the fullest, something I aspire to do, too. She taught me many profound truths: she taught me by example to love myself as I am, not as I would like to be; she taught me to not judge me for being me. She taught me to read the energy fields of others, like children do intuitively.

One thing rings true in my head and heart as her gifted mantra: "Jay, you are an innocent man, and I adore you, and everything else is just "stuff." Stuff is the details, the "dailies," the little annoyances we learn from as we go and grow and become our real selves.

When Shona walked into my life, I was bent, but not yet broken, by my own traumas of childhood and combat. Shona was unbreakable and unbroken. Such inspiring courage I had never seen in any other human.

My sister's daughter, Laura Chason Love, described Shona this way: "Shona saw electricity in everyday objects that are common yet unfamiliar to minds that don't relish in inner creativity…"

Shona also taught me about the reality of *truth*. "There is my truth," she said, "there is your truth, then there is what really happened." The strange thing is this: all three are true and all three are not true, all at the same time. We are all prejudicial in our memories. This, we concluded, is the nature of our quantum world.

Shona's childhood survival, as you will see, was incredulous even to me. This book is partly her testament in the court of the world. Wherever I could, I verified what she told me and I believed her every word. We never lied to each other, we never withheld our truth from each other, we never hurt each other with intention, and we never made each other wrong. That was the strength behind our success as best friends and life partners.

This book is the story of Shona's life before she met me, as she wrote it and told it to me. But the heart of this book is the story of us, a magical story of the impossible and incredible love we created and shared.

Yes, I, the author, am biased. I am a lover, not a fighter. And I loved her as you, dear reader, will discover.

— **Jay Harden**
Wentzville, Missouri
November 2020

Spirit on Fire

A Story of Love, Art & Healing

Chapter One

Meeting Shona:
The Day I Lost My Mind

We met by chance, or so it seemed,
September's chosen day;
a laugh, a smile, a lilting truth
compelled my Spirit stay.

The day I met Shona was the strangest day of my entire life, one that began in fear and ended up as an incredible awakening.

Most of the time, we do things we like and sometimes things we don't like. On rare days, people are compelled to do things that defy reason, as if they are forced by the great power of the universe. That Saturday in 1997 turned out to be a combination of all three.

That day I had already made two decisions. As I drove from Virginia to Georgia, I resolved to return to the cemetery, some 800 miles away, to complete my grieving for my beloved first wife, Carolyn. In my lifetime of traumas, the loss of Carolyn was the greatest of all. It was now exactly ten years after her untimely death, and time to finally release her from my heart.

I asked our children to meet me there, but destiny forced me to go alone. With many emotions percolating in and out of my consciousness, I drove south to the land of my birth, a slow and humid place still locked in ancient ways now foreign to me.

I had also resolved to confront and destroy an old unrelated fear of mine. All my life, I had been puzzled by the popularity of getting a massage. On my business trips I noticed that upscale hotels offered it and many times I peered in the door hoping to catch a glimpse, always accompanied by a slight shiver. I never dared go beyond thinking about what that experience was like.

I did not know that my profound fear of being touched by others originated in childhood, something I learned later when I was forced to deal with combat trauma from my time in Vietnam. But that day, before I lost my temporary courage, I resolved to turn and look this dragon in the eye. I did not want to go to my grave regretting any undone things, especially those based on fear.

I timed my trip in such a way that I could arrange my first massage en route to the cemetery. Today was the day: now or never. I was determined to get this off my plate and out of my mind forever.

I stopped near Atlanta and called a few masseuses that were in the phone book. I went through several until I came to an elegant voice that soothed me like hidden wisdom. She sounded safe in spite of a foreign accent, British I assumed. I scheduled an appointment two hours later, giving me time to case the location. When I drove to the horse farm and saw the long, winding dirt driveway past an open gate. I knew where to place my car heading downhill in case I needed to sprint out and escape.

The walk from my car to her door was the longest of my life. My legs hardly worked, as if drugged. I started hyperventilating, simultaneously cursing and bargaining with God, promising with great sincerity to become a monk, even a nun, if only I survived the day.

At exactly the point of no return, I noticed the black beast A large quiet dog stared at me, motionless, around the corner of the house as though assessing an attack. I decided to keep going, rather than retreat. I was not coming this close only to concede to some dark pet.

The Labrador walked slowly to intercept me. He seemed to have something in his jaws that looked like flesh. *Perhaps*, I thought, *a dismembered client of hers who did not fare well.* My mind was grinding, unable to make sense of the unfolding scene. He carried what looked like a rack of ribs. But where could that come from? Not off a grill, surely. Who gives a fresh rack of ribs to a dog? Any sensible dog would take his prize away to enjoy in a hidden place or bury it for later. My entire rational world was starting to crumble. Finally, he stopped, dropped the meat at my feet, then licked my hand.

From out of the air, I heard a lovely voice say, "Sage, no lick." This wonder dog, destined to help my healing, had made of me a sudden, unwilling friend. Together, we walked towards her. When I looked up, all I saw was this elegant figure framed in a golden halo of hair and a calm smile.

"You must be John."

Still speechless and looking around for a reality anchor, I barely nodded. She turned and swished her full-length colorful print dress and directed me inside.

I followed her downstairs to a small room (actually a former bomb shelter) lit by fragrant candles, hinting of incense. The massage table centered the room, with a day bed resting against the far wall. Soft music completed the creation of a separate world. I stammered to say that I had never done this before, hoping she would realize I needed advice. She told me to put my clothes on the chair and lay face down on the table while she went upstairs to turn off the answering machine.

When she left, my mind escaped control and I imagined cops bursting in the door to arrest a naked man. So I just stood there. When she returned I started undressing. Embarrassed, she left the room. After I assumed the position, I heard the door open. I could not see her with my face down and feet pointed toward the door. I didn't know if anyone else was in the room. My heart raced. All I could hear was the music and the occasional *plouf-plouf* of pumping massage oil.

At that moment, I started trembling. I wanted to be anywhere else in the world but here. My body was totally inflexible from fear and stress. She started chatting and I didn't know if a conversation was part of the process. I noticed things on the wall saying she was an ordained minister and performer in the 1996 Olympics. These incongruous things, perhaps warnings, were just not adding up. I was stuck in an intolerable situation of my own creation and she was blocking my only exit. Only a miracle of some sort could save my life.

She talked of Princess Diana with casual familiarity and told me incredible stories of her life, a life of privilege completely at odds with a massage on a farm in Georgia. When she told me she was an aviator, one of the first female hot air balloon pilots in England, that was my confirmation of disbelief. She didn't know I was on a B-52 crew in the Vietnam War and I wasn't about to challenge her incredible claims, not at the moment.

Her words began to blur into a continuous stream of rising and falling syllables I could no longer connect, a poetic litany fading and flowing over me, soothing all my fears, my thoughts.

Through some kind of divine guidance, her tenderness completely disarmed me. For the first time in my life, my mind just quit working, and I felt the strangest, most unexpected peace of my life. My brain simply filled to overflowing and gave up, unable to think though things any more. My ears drowned. For the only time in my life, my brain simply quit and went silent. For the first time, I was open to the universe and one with it, a part of all creation. I surrendered to something blissful, always sought, and unknown, and I was left as a new baby without experience or opinion, naked in the moment.

Her voice faded beyond translation and for some reason still unknown, I relaxed. My body simply yielded to her hands and voice and I gave up trying to understand what was happening, trying to control what I clearly had no control over at all. Then I must have lost my mind, that familiar part of me that always managed to keep me alive no matter what the circumstances.

In that moment, I knew for the first time ever what it felt like to be utterly safe in the perfect present, gently nudged by the voice and touch of this radiant being, this stranger. In that suspension of conventional time, I experienced the unveiled connection of the universe with me as one living whole. I'll never be sure exactly what happened, but I can fairly say it was a mystical experience of finding the real and authentic me.

As changed as a butterfly from a crawling caterpillar, I walked to my car. I heard a voice emerging from inside me. It said aloud, "I don't think I'm supposed to leave yet." The words flowed out effortlessly and by then I was no longer surprised at what I said or even her casual response.

"Oh," she said. "That happens all the time. Come sit on the couch for a while."

I did. She told me she was an artist and also a spiritual counselor as if these facts were an invitation. And completely without effort or my usual shyness, I told her every essential thing about my life, all due to the inexplicable trust we had just forged. I had found the right companion to walk with me and guide me in the process of becoming myself, another who would take my gifts in exchange for hers. At that moment, my life and hers turned to a new, brighter, and clearer direction, a moment we had both awaited, now slowly being shared.

I hope to step into that house again one day when the current occupants are away and install a small inconspicuous copper plate about four inches square into the flooring of that tiny significant room, one that simply says . . .

This is where
it happened
on September 22, 1997,
the moment
I lost my mind.

. . . the day I met Shona and our history began.

Chapter Two

Shona's Art

I remember you sitting
with a thousand colored pencils and pens
and expanses of inviting white,
deep in your creative spirit,
me silently privileged
to watch an unleashed goddess
directed by her divinity . . .

That day I couldn't help but notice the vibrant art displayed throughout Shona's home. She told me about it ever so casually, as if it were ordinary. It wasn't.

She called them "Sacred Geometries of God" and she was quick to remind me that it was not *her* art—she was simply the one who had been given it to put into tangible form. I was very impressed by the powerful, transformative nature of these luminous paintings.

Some of her works were spiritual portraits, some were depictions of divine laws, still others represented the highest vision of a company or business. Shona said that they were based on the right brain spatial languages of symbolism and color. By channeling these, she conveyed deep and meaningful messages straight to the heart as well as to the mind. As Shona explained:

These drawings serve as gateways and instruction manuals that take you deep into your divine blueprint, awakening and bringing into consciousness the divine codes you already possess. These patterns of love and light open up new dimensions of living consciously and in oneness with your inner I Am Presence. They invite you to BE, to come home to your beloved self, and to have the glorious life that is in store for you.

Shona was completely self-taught. She was denied proper schooling and never allowed to paint or draw as a child. She did not receive any professional training in design until she attempted art school at age 60 at Portfolio Center in Atlanta, Georgia. The school focused on preparing students for the commercial market. She left a few months later, feeling like a failure, after being told she did not possess the basic formal skills.

The calendar she was working on as an assignment at the time was composed of photos that I took of Shona, with original poetry and artwork by her. Four pieces of that work survive:

Feel The Earth

Oh! Sacred dance carry me,
Lift me, floating, soaring.
I join
The spinning galaxies that wrap the standing stones
In alternating spirals of light.
Hands and hearts are joined as we spin,
Creating the ancient druidic fires,
Igniting the sacred solstice pyres,
As the earth opens and rejoices.
In the stillness, silently, secretly, before the dawn,
Other sacred circles are found
Carved into the patchwork rills of wheat and rye by
Magical hands from some other plane.
They forge messages of love and beauty
For all mankind to see.
Ancient hieroglyphs older than man himself
Grace the fields of England's sacred lines.

I dance through circle after circle,
Ripples of cosmic energy touching my feet,
Melding heaven and earth in one vast arena.
And I, the dancer, hold them both in me
As the conduit of their unity.

Honor the Sacredness

A peace floods my being,
And ripples through my veins
As I ignite the fires of my soul's longing.
Time stands still,
Angels and demons hold hands
To dance a madrigal.
Moonbeams and starlight
Bend to touch the earth at my feet.
Then the sun folds into me and
Cosmic fire illuminates my being.
Incandescent flames of my heart's desire
Now burn into fulfilment.
I know who I am, and I am at peace.

Explore the Darkness

In the Spring, when flower blooms so sweetly
and birds herald the dawn with Divine voice,
They raped me, my father and my mother.
In the Spring, when life flows so abundantly
and joyously, freed from the confines of Winter,
I died with despair and pain every night.
They made me their slave and their concubine;
I had no other life.
Alone in the darkness, the only child in a world
of adults, in a world of war, gangrene and death.
I knew nothing of childhood;
I was a grown woman while yet a babe,
scarcely a few years old.
It was always a secret, always hidden,
never spoken of, never remembered,
Secret, under the niceties of the social graces,
Smiles, and polite conversation at the Viceroy's Palace.
Later, after a few more years of suffering, after
weeks of scurvy on a dark and dismal troop ship I died.
In the Spring I celebrate who I have become,
who I have always been, before they tortured me.

I have found my heart's desire.
In the Spring I dance with the fairies and the
flowers, I celebrate freedom, wisdom, and joy,
I am whole, real, and forever free.
I have walked through my terrible past into a
profoundly wonderful present;
I own my world, my awesome world, all of it,
the good and the bad of it.
It's all one anyway!
And I am so beautiful, powerful, and free.

Become the Wildness

Wild, unfettered wind blows through my hair,
Drifting leaves and twigs twist crazily in the air
Forming grotesque shapes and patterns.
Close to my body I feel it: grey fur,
Soft, silken depths of the wild, smells of
Damp deep earth, and fresh breezes lingering,
And my soul is caressed as we run together.
Ancient lineage and sacred animals are we
Together, woman and wolf.
We share the same soul, the same breath,

He and I
She and I.
As we lie down together under the trees,
Our hearts beat as one heart.
The pack comes over, curious, inquisitive.
Then all sit in the sacred silence
To commune wolf style,
Staring into some shared and distant
Wordless world.
Our eyes lock. I am transfixed, held lovingly,
Held closely, and gently bound.
I see through the knowingness of wolf.
My wildness becomes the connecting force
Of centuries of friendship.
I kneel in reverence and gratitude to be
Allowed to share this sacred and Divine rite.
In the oneness, I am deeply aware of my
Beautiful Goddess, of my essence,
And I am in awe of the power of me.

Whenever Shona worked on her art, it was by the direction of Divine Presence. Her hand was guided while she simply watched the art unfold. How and when she was called to create was not a mystery to Shona. As she told me, "I just know when I am to paint. The spiritual awareness I feel becomes a spatial awareness turned to shapes and bright colors."

I didn't truly understand what that meant until 1989 when she demonstrated her remarkable process. I watched her unroll art paper, take out her straight edges, French curves, colored pencils, crayons, marker pens and other media like glitter; then go into a meditative trance. While we both watched, her hand started drawing. I had to suspend my disbelief.

When I took out my camera and made some photographs, the strobe took her out of her spiritual connection and I never did that again, satisfied with the privilege of simply being a witness.

Shona considered her work a new form of art, calling it "Art for Vision." Her intent was to create art as a healing tool for insight, and for greater understanding of Self and others. She worked diligently to try to help people find what she described as their Inner Art Genius, at one point giving a series of workshops across the U.S. and Canada on "Art and the Ascension Process." She firmly believed that as children of God, we all have the power to create anything we can envision.

When people asked Shona to explain her art, she wanted them to find the meaning for themselves. Several people viewing a particular Shona drawing at the same time would share out loud what they saw in the work; sometimes they would nod at each other in agreement and other times would see completely different meanings. That seems to me to be the nature of the spiritual self-healing method her art offered.

And, of course, Shona found her own unique meaning in her art, too, because she clearly said it was not *her* art, but Spirit's art, and that she was merely the delivery system for it all.

Shona, being a spiritual counselor, pointed viewers of her art in the right direction by example. She often voiced what she believed the patterns in a particular work represented.

In the collection of Shona's art I inherited, I found two drawings dated May 5, 2013, the only ones I found annotated with her explanatory writing.

The first one she annotated as #1 Blueprint. It was a print of *Instruction for New Species*.

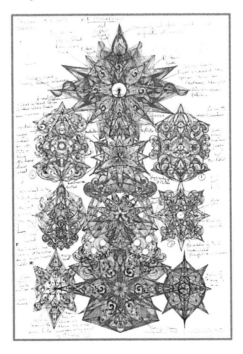

The second one she annotated as *#2 Instructions*. It was a print of *2008 Calendar New Species*.

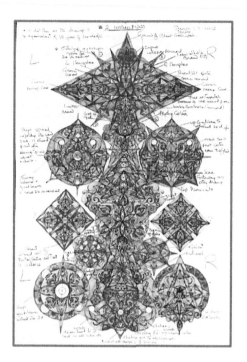

These two works are rare treasures. I am glad she left these specific drawings and annotations for us. They do serve to give some insight into Shona's creative and therapeutic processes, and her mysterious wisdom.

Shona had high hopes for her own artwork. Her divine inner wisdom told her they must go out into the world. She believed they had healing properties and wanted to hang them in doctors' offices just to see what might happen.

In January of 2001, she persuaded our minister, Reverend Carole O'Connell, at Unity North Atlanta Church, to hang her work in the sanctuary. It was the biggest piece she had done at the time, 32 feet long, called *The Journey of Mankind's Path Back Home. (Blueprint of the Christ Consciousness Within Each of Us)*.

The Journey of Mankind's Path Back Home
(Blueprint of the Christ Consciousness
Within Each of Us)

Shona worked from paper rolls of various widths, some up to 84 inches wide, primarily using crayons, marker pens, and colored pencils. Her largest piece measured 72 feet in length, taking almost three years to complete. Her works addressed new archetypes: the Divine Mother and the Divine Male, various interpretations of The Grail, and graphic journeys into healing, spirituality, and new knowledge.

Another large work, titled *The Way Here* is 6 x 16 feet long and was created in the summer of 1996. It depicts the 13 cycles of the Divine Feminine through drawings of male and female chalices. *The Venus*, a 4 x 6 feet piece, was one with intense personal significance that Shona kept in her bedroom.

The sizes of many of Shona's works discouraged reproduction and public display, limiting access to a wider audience, but they are extremely powerful and dynamic. Several videos show her explaining their significance.

Her output over the years was prodigious—she created close to a one hundred ethereal pieces that have been shared widely. Her work has a child-like quality to me, and some would consider it technically flawed, yet it has been displayed on a mountain top, in a church, in mansions, and in schools—anywhere she was guided to take them. I once tried to catalog them all for her, but it was hopeless. At first, she refused to sign her work, since it was not hers. She would not date them, either. Eventually, I did convince her to give them names.

Slowly, over time and by word-of-mouth, her art found a following, always evoking a wide variety of strong emotional reactions in her audience. People often felt a resonant energy presence and wanted to physically interact with the drawings, as Shona intended, trying to merge with them. Sometimes, they needed to walk directly upon them and when they did, some would weep with wordless joy, seeing and feeling things in the work no one else did. But the primary experience was a kind of spiritual healing—one that was, and is, highly unique to each observer. This is what compelled Shona to continue the art, even when she had financial difficulties.

Shona's cosmic vision extended way beyond her paintings. She longed to bring alternative and spiritual fields to the general public in a simple ordinary way. She dreamed of launching a television station that would cover all aspects of the newest trends in alternative healing and the metaphysical world that would encourage people to see how they could benefit from some of these ideas. She designed calendars, posters, and T-shirts so that these energy patterns could be available to all levels of income. This was important to her. She tried to sell T-shirts of her art at a sidewalk kiosk during the 1996 Olympics, but sales were poor. I suspect I have the one remaining shirt from that time, tattered and worn by love.

Soon I discovered that Shona was having a hard time supporting herself, her son, and her daughter from her massage work, spiritual counseling and art sales. Of course, all are unpredictable professions and have no benefits like health care or retirement.

I wanted to help. I knew that her greatest fear was to become homeless again, as she had once been while living in London, so I asked her if she would do my portrait. When I asked her what she charged, to my surprise, she did not know. She had a hard time pricing what she insisted was not her art, but something divinely guided. We settled on charging by the square foot based on the finished product. Then she asked me for a photo of myself when I was a child. I gave her a copy of my favorite.

Jay Harden | Age 6
© Olin Mills Photography

She said she would meditate on it. A month or more passed as I waited with anticipation. Then, Shona said it was ready. The finished portrait was 48 x 40 inches and the price was $400. Part of that portrait is the cover of this book.

**Jay Harden
with *Portrait of J Harden***
© Camilla Carolyn Collins

Seven years later, when I moved to Missouri in late 2006, I framed it myself and hung it above my fireplace. It is still vibrant, though it has faded from ambient light. I wrote to Crayola asking how to preserve artwork created with their crayons (made mostly of clay). They sniffed back a non-answer that crayons are not intended to be permanent art!

Portrait of J Harden still dominates my house today. Each time I look upon it with intent, I see new intimate things not there before, such as my complexity, my curiosity, my warrior past, the light of me, and other hidden gifts. It is still somewhat hard for me to imagine being so spiritually powerful and beautiful as a human. It humbles me and gives me hope. It brings me back into the moment, and the everyday noise of the day drifts away.

I recently found a painting of Shona's on eBay listing for $13,500. Were she still alive, I believe that Shona would have made a good living from her art, but monetary gain was never at the heart of

21

what she did purely out of love and reverence for the evolution of all humanity.

In 2011, when after years of denials and appeals I was awarded my 100% disability from the VA, I told Shona I was giving it all to her for the rest of her life, about $33,000 a year. I knew that I could never repay her for saving my life many times so we could live and love together, and I wanted her to be secure financially so her great fear of homelessness and poverty as a bag lady in London would fade.

Life is funny, you know, or as she would say, our lives are guided by the universe. Now that Shona has left this life, that money came back to me as her gift. And with that money I was able to buy my present home, near my daughter, where it is quiet and peaceful, just what I needed to write her story undisturbed, just as she knew I would.

Chapter Three

Shona's Childhood

Her hair a field of flowers,
she plays away the hours,
skipping when she walks.
She giggles as she talks.
Wonder is her way of living every day.

Shona possessed an amazingly open, trusting, buoyant spirit—that was clear to me from the very moment we met. It would be impossible to fathom the depth of Shona's courage, her creativity, and her desire to heal others without knowing something of her highly traumatic early history.

Shona was born in New Delhi, India, on April 4, 1941, to John Edward Mercer Ewart Clark Leask (Ewart) and Deirdre Jean Laird Leask. She was baptized at Christ Church in Simla, India.

Her parents gave her a Gaelic name, 'Shonagh,' which means enchanted one or bringer of great joy, but the silent *gh* was dropped. As British landed gentry, her mother and father were not expected to raise their own children, so Shona's first language was Hindustani, learned from her *Ayahs*, her Indian nannies.

Lieutenant John Edward Mercer "Ewart" Clark Leask
& Deirdre (Laird) Leask | December 18, 1934
Unknown Photographer

Christ Church | Simla, India
Unknown Photographer

Shona's mother clearly was unhappy about not having birthed a male heir to the Leask line, and motherhood in general. As Shona relates:

> *Mother was horrified that I was a girl. 'Don't want it, put it back.' She never connected with me again. I was badly neglected and hated. After a month, we went to the mountains with the spring exit from Delhi. The rough handling and distancing I get is so shocking that the real me leaves the body never to come back. There is no one there. I am all alone, nobody ever answers me when I cry. I scream a lot, but it does not seem to make a difference, so I just stop and switch off.*

Shona Darley Leask, July 12, 1941, Simla, India

Shona as an Infant
Unknown Photographer

Both Shona's mother and her father were heavy drinkers, most likely alcoholics, and Shona clearly and vividly remembers the horror of being continuously sexually abused by them as a toddler, as well as by other members of their family. In one incident, her godfather, Major Stanley Henry James Whitehead, known as Zulu, tied her down and victimized her. Instead of being comforted or

25

tended to, Shona is blamed for this by her mother when she finds out. In another instance, Zulu abuses her and then tries to smother her with a pillow. As this occurred, Shona recalls:

> *I don't understand why I don't die. I long to die. After passing out, I come to alone lying on the floor, I don't cry. I am too numb. I just get into bed.*

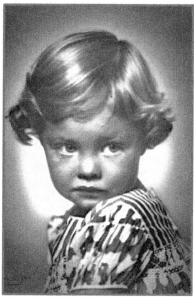

Shona at Age 2
Unknown Photographer

Sometime during that same year, Shona suffers another traumatic event.

> *I get found by three Indian officers when I was hiding in the rocks up the hills. They had huge knives and they pinned me down and one by one raped me. I didn't even struggle.*
>
> *I already knew that it would be no good, so I let it happen. I went back to camp and did not say a word because they said that they would kill me, and I believed them as they would have lost their commissions if I told.*

Shona's father was then a Lieutenant-Colonel in Britain's Indian army. While her father was away at war, Shona was at the mercy of Deirdre.

> *Mother was always drunk and many nights I went to bed hungry. One night, she came back even more drunk than usual and tried to kick me to death. She locked me into a little room with no windows, so I hear only street noises. I have no loo, no refrigerator, and no food for days and days. I was starving. She woke from another drunk and went nuts. She suddenly slung me hard against the wall and knocked me out, cracking open my head, which bled. In the morning, it seems the blood brought her to her senses.*

When she was almost three years old, her father was killed in a grenade ambush while serving at the front. Deirdre told Shona she caused his death and she believed it was her fault.

Deirdre, in her frequent letters to her mother, admits to being a reluctant parent.

One night Shona's mother checked into the Ritz Hotel in Bombay. They went to the room and Shona was locked in while her mother went to the new desk clerk that evening and took another room for herself.

For three days, Shona drank from the tap and had no food while her mother was gone.

What happened after Deirdre returned was beyond terrifying for little Shona.

> *I think my mother realized that she was going to really kill me. Without saying anything, she simply handed me over to some colleagues at the British embassy and I saw a ship and the sea for the first time. My mother had put me on a troop ship bound for Africa.*
>
> *I thought I was dying and leaving the world as we sailed away. The two people who were in charge of me avoided me as much as possible. I had very little food and soon got very ill on*

the boat. While lying still in a bundle of dirty blankets, a soldier tripped over me, calling me a piece of rubbish.

Then I knew it was true. I was worthless. Shortly afterwards, a crazy, dirty man, who had been eying me for days, carried me into a secluded part of the ship and raped me. I did not care. He and I were the same.

My body was leaving as I was dying. Up through the mists, I saw the tunnel, only to be turned back. Not even God wanted me. The rest of me just never came back. Only a sentient being came back and lived for decades as me.

I arrive in Cape Town many weeks later, with no hair and deathly ill from scurvy.

Shona's ship landed in Cape Town on November 14, 1943. Her maternal grandmother, Ethel Wright Laird, still had not been notified of her arrival and so Shona spent several weeks in an orphanage. There, she was abused by one of the nuns by being given chocolate laxatives as a punishment—a psychological injury that had life-long repercussions for Shona and her final illness. When her grandmother was finally located, Shona went to live with her and her grandfather, retired Brigadier Kenneth Macgregor Laird, at High Hedges on Kenilworth Road.

My grandmother was a great society beauty and was horrified at having to take care of me. She made it her personal goal to feed me up and glamorize me into the perfect little girl.

My grandfather hated me and was furious that I had been sent to them without warning, He was cruel and mean but my grandmother was the first person to seemingly love me. At least she put me to bed, read me stories, and spent some time with me.

I had a black nanny but she only helped my grandmother. I had a dear, dear friend who was the man who came to clean our cars. He was kind and respectful to me. We would talk for hours.

Then one day, the same old thing happened with my grandfather. It frightened me and I ran in to tell my grandmother to tell him to stop. She acted very weirdly and kept telling me not to worry. A doctor came and examined me.

Here Shona is describing what she later related to me. Her grandfather raped her and forced her to masturbate him. Once, he was standing behind his big desk chair when his wife came in. He told her to get Shona away from him. He zipped up without being seen and Shona was again blamed for instigating her own abuse. In another situation, beyond comprehension to a child, Shona took on the shame of causing another's death.

Granny Laird & Shona at Age 1
Unknown Photographer

I loved the cook, Spizer. He got me out of trouble many times. He fed me, then everything started to go crazy. Three police cars came and took him away. No amount of crying or pleading made any difference. No one mentioned it until months later when my grandmother said that I was now safe because he had been put to death for molesting a white child.

That was when I knew that I was a murderer. I vowed that I would never use my female power again for anything. I would be a boy like my mother wanted. I spat on the earth and changed forever.

Then my grandmother said that it was time I grew up and stopped dancing and lying about fairies. She took my gramophone and found me a governess. Appalled that I was left-handed, she

*tied my hand behind me. I went to a fancy school called Herschel
in Cape Town, UGH.*

From my own experience with incest at a very early age, I
know how reasonable it is for a child to assume they are at fault.
Shona's experience and conclusion that she could be responsible for
another's death were repeated in this country by Oprah Winfrey and
Maya Angelou. (Angelou thought it was her voice that caused the
death of others and she became mute for almost five years.)

As Shona's abuse continued, Shona's mother was busy
traveling and husband hunting and did not rejoin her in Cape Town
until some two years later in May of 1945. Deirdre wrote her mother-
in-law, Mamoushka, to say, "It was really a lovely day and very hot
and the beach was grand. Unfortunately, it was very high tide and
there was little sand, but S. and I paddled and she simply loved it."
At this time Shona was not afraid of the sea.

Shona told me details of her relationship with her
grandfather, the Brigadier. Once he took her by the hand for a walk.
Shona loved the kittens that populated High Hedges. He instructed
her to pick up the kittens and put them in a bag. After the bag was
full of mewing kittens, he tied the top and took Shona to a lake. There
he forced her to throw the bag into the water. Shona was traumatized
for being a kitten murderer, too. But that was not the worst.

He took her to the beach. She was playing in the surf as he
watched from his chair. Shona was probably pulled by a rip tide.
Drowning, she screamed for help. Her grandfather pretended not to
hear her, but a black woman did. She was nearby on the black-only
section of the beach. If she had crossed over and rescued Shona she
knew she would have been killed, so she could do nothing but
scream, too. Fortunately for Shona, a white man behind her
grandfather understood her danger and saved Shona's life that day.
For as long as I knew her, when we went to Hilton Head, Gulf
Shores, the Outer Banks, or any beach, she rarely ventured into the
ocean.

When Shona was seven, her mother remarried. Ivan Kaufman was a lawyer, and Shona went to live with them in Zimbabwe, where she was brought up in affluence as a Jewish young lady, side-by-side with both white and black cultures. As Shona would later write:

> I went to the Synagogue, learnt about God and the Bible. We went on safari a lot to a ranch in Gwello which was my father's and to Gwanda which I think belonged to the Kaufman family. We played a lot in the garment warehouses and lived a very rich life.
> I loved the black people and tried to spend as much time as I could with them.

Shona learned to track and to hunt Guineafowl, and became a reliable shot with a .22 rifle. She was strictly trained in the art of the kill and the responsible protection of the wild. If she (or anyone) wounded an animal, they had to track it down and not let it say wounded

> It was the bush that I loved and the Matobo Mountains. I loved the snakes and the wild animals. On the ranches, the natives still lived in their old villages and were so kind to children. From them I learned to listen to the earth and the wind, to smell their signs and obey them if I wanted to stay alive.

Her stepfather became a circuit judge, traveling for six weeks at a time, which allowed Shona to spend much of her childhood steeped in ethnic African village life. Shona grew up listening to storytellers from the Kalahari and Zulu traditions. She also saw, and was saddened, by the injustices of segregation and discrimination.

> I remember that once a year there would be a great celebration when the storyteller would come to town. He looked like no other African I had ever seen, small with a wide flat face, shining eyes and very tightly curled white hair, he would have the

31

whole village enraptured sitting around the fire and would talk of his land, and his stories.

How I wish I could have recorded those stories. It was only until many years later that I realised that I was one of the last white people to ever meet with a Kalahari bushman—their race died out because they would not allow themselves to be enslaved or captured. They were so powerful they would just die. They were children of the wild and freely beaten.

We knew who the chief was and we respected him greatly, but he never used his station to be grand or to wield unfair power. If we ever did something wrong, someone would sit down with us and talk to us, and help us to see why it was not appropriate. I loved being there but could only do it while my parents were away.

Shona at Age 3   **Shona at Age 8**
Unknown Photographer

When she was 10, Shona's family moved to England, where she attended private schools and lived a life of relative aristocratic ease, with vacations in Europe and frequent trips to visit her grandmother in Ireland, including one summer holiday in Rhodesia where she witnessed firsthand the growing inequities of apartheid.

As a young woman, Shona hoped to become a concert pianist. When she was 16, she studied piano, harp, and voice at The Guildhall School of Music in London. Her training, which required her to practice seven hours each day, was suddenly cut short. At age 17, she was sent to finishing school in the evenings to be trained as a debutante to be presented to Queen Elizabeth II, at the last court event of its kind.

At finishing school, the girls were taught the structure and ranks of the aristocracy, proper etiquette, and how to walk, talk, dress, smile and curtsy. Shona's physical trans-formation to a debutante was phenomenal in those few months. Here are the photos of her when she started and finished:

Shona at Age 16   **Shona at Age 17**

Unknown Photographer

Despite all the restrictions on young women in 1958, in her diary Shona wrote:

Was presented to the Queen and had a garden party at Buckingham Palace. I wore a dress of blue carnations and spoke to HM. Loved the palace, hated the ceremony. We partied every night had lunch parties every day, went to Ascot, Queen Charlotte's Ball, and all the other appropriate social events. My photo was in The Tatler, and the gossip columns had a field day. I discovered a cafe called the Mardi Gras in South Kensington where I would run away to and talk existentialist conversations.

On Sundays when I could run away, I went to Cy Laurie's Jazz Club in a basement in Soho London, for five hours we would dance without stopping, Dixieland Jazz was all the rage. We had great performers, Louis Armstrong, and others.

My mother found out and all outings came to an end. My chaperoning became even stricter. I lost one of my friends to an illegal abortion. We had to go with her to a seedy part of town— awful, we felt so dirty and wrong.

Shona had her coming out on the staircase at Highclere Castle (the setting of Downton Abbey). As she mentions, the debutante events were covered by *The Tatler* and its photographers. The magazine, begun in 1901, is now considered to be the first social media. Its focus was on high society lifestyle, fashion, and politics.

Up to that point, Shona was a proper English young lady kept completely ignorant of the workings of the real world. All decisions were taken from her and made for her. Her mother even hired her own nanny out of retirement, Nanny Simpson, to help in Shona's control. Shona said Nanny Simpson dressed her every day until her wedding. Shona was innocent of any knowledge about finances or basic sexuality. Although Shona exhibited a great intellectual curiosity all her life, she was given only the minimum education. She was not allowed to go to college to prevent her economic independence of men.

The primary purpose of the debutante season, of course, was to secure a suitable marriage. Shona's mother wanted her to marry a duke or an earl and she had given her a list of six acceptable suitors. Roderic Knowles was decidedly not on that list. Roderic was an Irish wild child and true to his character, he seduced Shona during the debutante season.

Shona then felt ill. She complained and her mother took her to a doctor on Sloan Street. He said, "She has morning illness; she is two months pregnant." Shona had no idea. She had no preparation for this possibility, and thought she was responsible.

And so, Shona's childhood abruptly came to an end.

Chapter Four

Shona's Marriages

In giving is not loss, but gain;
through our gifts we mute the pain
of others waiting for their time
to sing with us that peaceful rhyme of love,
the power shared by all
when we attend its sacred call.

Roderic Marshall Knowles

In the cab ride home from the doctor's office, Shona's mother started screaming, "How could you? Just wait until we get home!"

There she started beating Shona with a broom. "You've ruined my life, everything! You don't deserve anything. You ruined your body. You will never be acceptable by the world, never get anywhere!" This physical and verbal abuse went on for two hours. Shona further internalized her belief that she destroyed other people by word and deed.

That night Deirdre told Shona to get rid of it and gave her a knitting needle and a bottle of gin. Shona didn't know what to do.

She poured the bottle in her lap and couldn't understand the purpose of the knitting needle. Her baby was saved.

Then Deirdre went to Lady Swinfen (the wife of Roderic's stepfather) to force Roderic to marry Shona. The two exchanged tirades, but finally agreed on the necessity of marriage. Shona and Roderic had no say about it.

Shona at Her Wedding to Roderic | March 1959
Unknown Photographer

And so, on March 18 of 1959 at St. Columba's Church of Scotland in Chelsea, Shona and Roderic were married. Shona was forbidden to wear white. Their son, James Andrew Ivan Knowles, was born September 12th that same year. According to Shona: "They bound my breasts. I did not know breast feeding existed."

With little income and no help from their parents, Shona and Roderic got a cheap apartment. Shona struggled without a nanny, the only kind of motherhood she ever knew, and Roderic revealed his wildness. He drank into the night and brought his friends home. Shona often woke up in the morning with strange men passed out in her bed.

By day, Roderic worked as an apprentice accountant and dreamed of being an artist. Roderic finally quit the firm and with help from his mother, Lady Swinfen, Shona and Roderic opened an art gallery on Sloan Street. Shona ran the Gallery. But despite having aristocratic patrons, they struggled to make it. They were very poor.

"I was not used to living in poverty and found it very hard," said Shona. "I really had no idea how to manage my life or that of a child. Eighteen-year-olds do not make the best parents, especially then. We were so protected that we had no life experience like today."

The marriage became intolerable to her. It was clear to Shona that Roderic didn't care at all about her or the baby. She left Roderic in May of 1960 when James was eight months old and she divorced him in late 1964.

When Shona told me about Roderic early on in our relationship, I got a used copy of his 1972 book, *The Great Bank of America Telex Heist: A True Adventure,* written by Roderic while he was in a Dutch prison. I read it to see if Shona was mentioned. Thankfully, she was not. He tells of his international smuggling of gold bars in a custom designed coat (he includes instructions) with a projected profit of $4,000,000 a year. Then he said, "[this] was a confidence man's dream: a bold plan to rob the Bank of America of $600,000 in just two days without guns, masks, or holdup notes." And that is what he did. He called himself "a most uncommon criminal."

Roderic later became interested in yoga and, like me, went to India at another ashram to study with Swami Muktananda, then proceeded to re-clothe his original self. "Truth at any cost," he declared once, "I will not cease until I find it." He was convincing and believed by many, but not me.

I recently went to Roderic Knowles' current website, *www.roderickknowles.com,* and was astounded to see his list of published books, notable for the omission of his robber memoir. He now claims to be a cosmic philosopher, practical mystic, and esoteric teacher of wisdom. In my view, his website is full of self-adulation and smooth as a mellophone on Ex-Lax. He still has no idea of Shona's triumphs over trauma.

After leaving Roderic, Shona and James first tried to live with her grandmother (Brigadier Laird's widow) in Ireland. That lasted for two months. Even with their maid, Alice, Granny Laird, now 82, could not deal with an infant.

Desperate, Shona called her mother. Deirdre, too, hated her only child and told her so throughout Shona's childhood and her entire life. In fact, as Deirdre lay dying, Shona asked her to say, "I love you" just one time. Her mother refused. Shona asked her why and Deirdre said, "Because, my dear, it simply would *not* be true."

Within a few hours of the arrival of Shona with James, Deirdre said she was going to have Shona declared an unfit mother. She took James from Shona and threw her out with only the clothes on her back saying, "I never want to see you again!" Deirdre now had the boy she always wanted instead of Shona.

Shona lived in the basement boiler room until the building superintendent found her and confiscated her key. At age 19, Shona became a homeless bag lady. For the first time, Shona was truly alone, without a home or nanny, and it was wintertime in London.

She wandered the streets until she found a standing ruin from The Blitz in South Kensington, off King's Gate. The sign had these warnings: DANGER, BOMBED OUT, CONDEMNED, TO BE DESTROYED. Shona had found her first shelter. Out of shame, she stayed inside all day, going out only at night to raid the garbage of a nearby bakery for food.

Soon enough, a druggie found her place to shoot up. He raped Shona at knife-point. Shona had to move to the parks, sleeping at night on benches and cardboard.

One day, the police took her in for vagrancy. Before booking, in walked Shona's stepfather, Ivan. Still a practicing lawyer, he was looking for his client. Ivan was astonished. "What are you doing here?" Shona explained her situation. "Your mother told me you were living with friends!" he said. Ivan paid the rent for an attic apartment on Queen's Gate in Kensington and Chelsea, but gave Shona no money for food. He told her to get a job.

Shona, without any marketable skills, started looking for work, any work, even scrubbing floors at Fortnam & Mason where she later had a gold credit card, but her aristocratic voice betrayed her. She was told, "Go back to your own kind. You want to take a job from a decent working girl." A later irony occurred after Shona entered the aristocracy as Richard Bellew's wife. When she shopped there, the staff deferred to her cultured voice.

Shona hit the lowest point in her life: no family, no friends, no baby, no reason to keep living. Shona learned from trashed newspapers that Marilyn Monroe had just committed suicide, so she tried the same. By the most unbelievable coincidence, Shona had left her front door ajar. A drug addict who was looking for money for his next fix found her, then revived her. Fearing he would be blamed, he disappeared after calling the police. Shona's life was saved by the very man who had raped her in the bombed-out building!

Shona was hired as an Addressograph machine operator, but was fired for incompetence. During that time, she taught herself to use a typewriter. She was hired as a typist, but fired after a few weeks for her poor spelling.

On the street, she was approached and offered a job as a model. At a subsequent party, she met Richard Bellew, a man who was to change the course of the next 25 years of her life.

Richard George Bellew

In 1964, Shona began living with Richard. An only child, Richard told his father he wanted to marry Shona. Sir George, his father, became part of the nobility when he was appointed by Queen Elizabeth to be Garter King of Arms and became Lord Bellew and his wife, Ursula Kennard Cull, became Lady Bellew.

As head of the College of Arms, Sir George Bellew investigated Shona's family, the Leasks. He found Shona came from the Vikings of Norway through the Orkney Islands, then Scotland. He told Richard she was of suitable blood to marry.

The Queen inquired of Sir George about the wedding. Sir George said it would be held at Brompton Oratory in London. She replied, "Nonsense, George, you can use my private chapel at Windsor." They married on January 15, 1965. With her marriage to Richard, Shona advanced from landed gentry to the aristocracy and access to the Royal Household. She entered Burke's Peerage and DeBrett's Peerage where you can still find her today.

Shona does not remember much of the wedding ceremony, except she wore the same gold dress and hat in the portrait that artist Terence Cuneo painted. The social rage at the time was James Bond. This is clear from the engagement photos of the couple.

Later, Shona and Richard actually went gambling with Ian Fleming.

> *Our engagement party was held in London at the Inner Temple. Mother was furious that I had landed such a catch, considering I was spoiled goods! We then spent the [wedding] night at the Connaught Hotel in London, exhausted. We left on the Orient Express the next day for Gstaad and had a party on the platform. I wore a fabulous white fox coat.*
>
> *The trip on the train was interrupted all the time, but we had a luxury suite to ourselves. I almost got lost at breakfast as the train divided in half. I was on one and Richard had stayed in the breakfast car on the other half. We ran like mad along the platform.*
>
> *On our honeymoon Sir Winston Churchill died and we defied Papa by not going to his funeral which Papa planned.*

Shona remembered meeting Churchill when he and Sir George were planning his funeral. Shona found Churchill typically gruff and unpleasant.

Richard Bellew
& Shona (Leask) Bellew
1965
Unknown Photographer

Furious at their missing the funeral, Sir George thereupon disinherited Richard, meaning that he would no longer be given a living allowance. For the first time, Richard had to earn a living.

Richard found a job with I.B.M. which was to take them to Paris and twice to America, redirecting the trajectory of their lives and allowing the independent heart of Shona to blossom.

For 25 years, Shona was a loyal wife, adding to the Bellew line with three wonderful children. She was a dutiful partner, as she was trained to be. That was all she knew and that was why she had her children raised by nannies, like her. In her mind, Shona was not neglecting her children. As an aristocrat's wife, Shona was powerless. Out of love, she did all she could for her children within that social system, but it wasn't enough.

After a while, she was not content to stay at home, throw dinner parties, and be a socialite, so she let her hidden free spirit take her adventuring across the world—racing, singing, acting, dancing, making music, and other things. Later during our relationship, Shona and I were saddened to learn that the children felt neglected during that time. They believed that Shona was responsible for the breakup of their family, when her true intention was to save them (and herself) from an upper class English life.

Shona knew her children needed to be in alternative schools to thrive. Richard expected the boys to attend Eton like he and his father did. But Shona felt the kids were too American to be accepted into that stiff upper lip and severe hazing tradition. Shona desperately wanted to mother her children in a better, different way than she had been. For example, she and her kids did "boats." "Boats" was a happy evening together. They would move two couches face-to-face, forming a boat. They then piled in with plenty of popcorn and watched a marathon of VHS movies, talking and laughing.

Over the course of their marriage, Shona learned that Richard had several mistresses. One of them was Adin's nanny. Shona was no longer dutiful enough to stand this any longer. She confronted Richard. According to her, his reply went something like this: "How dare you bring that up! That's none of your business! Don't you ever mention it to me again!"

Shona was gaining her independent personal power and considered leaving their marriage. She consulted her uncle, Lieutenant-General Sir Henry Leask, about a divorce, the first by a Bellew wife in the history of Richard's line. Uncle Henry kindly advised her not to divorce Richard, just to live in separate parts of the house and to get herself a little "nookie" on the side.

When Shona told Richard of her intention, he threatened to gain custody of the children. Serena was 20 and in college in London, Fred was 17, and Adin was 9 at the time. This really shook Shona, defeating her plans to save them from the aristocratic life. But her growing inner wisdom prevailed and she cleverly called his bluff. Richard took the children to live with him while Shona moved out. She bravely waited for what she predicted and hoped. In a few weeks of failed parenting, Richard returned the children to Shona, a defeated father.

After their divorce was final on February 14, 1990, Shona left for the United States with Adin.

Raymond Leroy Cisco

In 1991, Shona came back to the U.S. as a single parent to work for The National Academy of Integrative Learning in Rochester, New York. With Peter Kline and his group, she presented seminars on Integrative Learning for Eastman Kodak.

In March of 1992, she visited Delphi University, a center for healing in McCaysville, Georgia. This is where she met Raymond, who was taking care of the guests staying there. Her first impression of him was quite positive.

> *He was very thoughtful, and helpful to me. I also had a chance to observe him giving counseling to some other people. They spoke highly of his ability to assist them. I was quite impressed,*

for not only was he kind and seemingly a good counselor, but I thought that he was a very beautiful and gentle person as well.

Shona decided to take the required classes to become an ordained minister and to practice as a spiritual counselor, commuting on a regular basis from her home in Rochester. Although they were not able to spend much time together, she and Raymond became close intimate friends. They seemed to have a lot in common. Sometimes Shona would bring her son Adin with her and both he and Raymond liked each other. Shona observed that Raymond was very kind and loving and gentle with her son.

In August of 1992, Raymond proposed and Shona enthusiastically accepted. According to Shona's daughter, Serena, Shona had an ulterior motive: marriage to an American would mean she qualified for a green card. When Shona arrived in the U.S., she hired an immigration lawyer to help her gain citizenship. He took her money but never advanced her case. She discovered later from his secretary that he was a dysfunctional alcoholic and had defrauded her. Her visa had expired by then and she was technically an illegal immigrant.

Shona and Raymond wed at Delphi at the end of August, although due to an error in their paperwork, their marriage actually became official on September 9, 1992.

During that time, Raymond wanted to travel to Brazil to study some special healing methods. They couldn't afford two tickets, so Shona and a few other students gave Raymond the money as a wedding gift. When he returned, Shona noticed that something was wrong.

I do not know what went on in Brazil, but there seemed to be a different attitude from Raymond after his return. He seemed to have upset several people on the tour. I inquired and was told that he had run up several phone bills which he could not pay. He had also drunk a lot and had caused an upset in the hotel.

I was very concerned, as I had not seen any of this behavior before. He explained that the country had been very strange and

45

that it had affected him emotionally, so he felt nervous and out of control. Knowing Brazil, that made a lot of sense. He apologized, paid the money back, and said it would not happen again.

He also shared with me the details of his childhood, and I learned for the first time that he had a criminal record. At first, I was shocked, but had seen him try so hard to put it all behind him and lead a new life. Delphi was also willing to give him another chance. I was happy to be married to him.

He completed his training as a minister and became very focused on his work. He was so proud of himself to have achieved something that was good and useful to society. The day of his ordination was very powerful for him and we were all thrilled to support him. It seemed as if he had everything.

In early 1992, Shona bought a plot of land within the Delphi community, paying them to build a house for her there where she and Raymond would live and share the mortgage. She moved to Delphi in January of 1993 and they rented various houses until her property was finished. Raymond, though still kind, seemed to grow more and more distant from her.

That March there was a fierce blizzard. With great kindness and patience, Raymond dealt with the different disasters. Shona and the Delphi community could not have survived half so well without Raymond's help. He seemed to be his old self again, and so he and Shona went on as if nothing had happened.

A short while later, a very large sum of money went missing from the Delphi office. At first the director, Patricia, asked all of those with children if the children had taken the money, but when all of them denied it, they had to look elsewhere. When Patricia asked Raymond if he had taken the money, he went off the wall. He was furious. He said that he was insulted and felt used by Delphi and that he was going to leave the community.

To Shona's despair, he simply left. Days went by and they heard nothing. Meanwhile, the police had been notified, but there was no proof. Then a few days later, someone cashed two Delphi checks at the local gas station. It proved to be Raymond.

I couldn't believe it—it was as if he meant to sabotage everything. His life was going so smoothly, and he was building a good client base. He had made a deep connection to his inner spirit. Why? I cried and cried, as I felt helpless and very confused.

I questioned not only my own judgment, but also that of Delphi, also. Were we all being cheated, as the local probation officer kept insisting?

Finally, the police picked him up, as if he was trying to be caught. He was taken to the Fannin County Jail where we tried to arrange some therapy for him. We tried to get him to explain what had happened. He continued to get angrier and angrier, blaming the center for his imprisonment, blaming the probation officer, and blaming everyone else.

I learned that he had been previously convicted for aggravated assault and was already on probation. I went to see Bobby Dills, the probation officer, to see if I could help him, but there was nothing I could do. Raymond was angry and felt that I had not done enough. He was sentenced to three months in a labor camp and then three months at the Blairsville Correctional Center.

Raymond served his time at the labor camp without any trouble, but after only a few weeks at Blairsville, he left his work detail for a day to visit Shona in McCaysville. Unfortunately, she was out that day and he bought some beer, got drunk, and turned up at someone's house, who called the police. He was then taken back to Fannin County Jail where he remained for quite a while.

He was finally charged with violating probation again and trying to escape. He faced 10 years, but Shona managed to get a lawyer, Robert Ballew, to represent him at the hearing. His term was reduced to five years. It was the best the lawyer could do, but Shona felt it was unfair. She didn't believe that Raymond was planning to escape because he could have returned to the center before curfew, if he hadn't been picked up by the police. As she later lamented:

He seems to always sabotage his life just when things are beginning to work out for him. This daunts me the most, for I wonder if it is possible to ever have a loving relationship with someone who always blames others and is constantly sabotaging

47

his life. Yet, there seems so much in him that is good. I am the only person who has a connection with him at all.

After less than three years of marriage, Shona divorced Raymond in May of 1995. It was uncontested, on the grounds that she unknowingly married a criminal. He died on December 22, 2011 of accidental drug overdoses. Shona had no idea that Raymond had a drug problem.

It was not the first time Shona had been deceived—it was her nature to be unconditionally loving and trusting of others—but most people she met from then on were unaware of her marriage to Raymond, as she was very ashamed of having been tricked into marrying yet another con man.

Shona | November 2011

Chapter Five

Shona
& Motherhood

**Splendid is our living
and the loving we created,
a thing that will endure
long after our bodies
have melted away.**

Shona adored her children and was determined that they not suffer the kind of traumatic childhood she had endured.

Shona wrote me an email in December of 1999 after we discovered our common destiny. The subject line was *Children Believe*. In it she said:

> *Children believe in miracles. They wait in their 'lost' time zone dreaming of being rescued, taken away from their misery by an archetypal figure, Jesus, angels, or somebody.*
>
> *It can happen if you give it to them, for you are the Christ and the Warrior. You can rescue all your lost children and bring them home. 'Suffer the little children to come unto me and forbid them not for theirs is the kingdom of heaven.'*

Bring <u>all</u> your kids home and you will be living in heaven and know the kingdom of God for it is your natural state of being. It has to be so.

When you rescue the wounded children, then you are healed of duality, judgment, and sin, and all that is left is God I AM. The mystery of life is solved and you become the conscious master of <u>all</u> your world.

No one is exempt—not any murderer or rapist—no one. We are all God I AM, deeply or less deeply wounded.

If anyone knew, Shona and I knew this: what can be more valuable than a safe childhood? And, as Shona would come to know, as I did, nothing is more tragic than losing a child.

James Knowles

Self Portrait by James Knowles

James Andrew Ivan Knowles, the eldest of Shona's four children, was born in London on September 12, 1959. When Shona's husband, Roderic, quit work as an accountant trainee and his parents stopped his housing allowance, he had to return home to live. Roderic's parents blamed Shona for getting pregnant and no such invitation was extended to Shona and their grandson.

Shona first tried living with Granny Laird, now a widow in Ireland, but it was too small a place and neither she or Alice, the ancient maid, could cope with a baby. In desperation, Shona turned to her mother for help. Deirdre had little compassion for the daughter she never wanted. As mentioned earlier, Deirdre wasted no time in declaring Shona an unfit mother and keeping James to raise, then one-and-a-half years old. Shona lived in dire straits, from hand-to-mouth, until she met her future husband, Richard Bellew, an aristocrat with impeccable lineage.

Shona's marriage to Richard brought stability and prosperity to Shona's life. James' two half-brothers and one half-sister were born between 1969 and 1980. From 1972 to 1975, James was sent by Deirdre to Stowe School, a prestigious boarding school favored by the aristocracy to become a proper English gentleman. It was the same boarding school attended by Richard Branson. During this time, James experimented with Molotov Cocktails and was caught by the Thames River Police speeding their boat, 'Smoody Blue.'

After living in Connecticut for eight years, Shona and Richard returned to the U.K. with their children Fred and Adin, living in a 17th-century thatched roof cottage on Slad Road in Stroud, Gloucestershire, England.

There she got a phone call from Interpol first, then detectives in the Stamford, Connecticut Police Department. They had been searching for her. Did she know a Jamie London? "Yes," she told them. "My son, James Knowles, goes by that name."

James also used the name Andrew DeKnowles, and earned his livelihood as an artist, sign painter, graphic designer, and motorcycle mechanic. He specialized in painting motorcycles.

They told her that James was dead, a victim of murder on September 23, 1989. Since she was next of kin, they asked her to come and identify his body. They were very kind and paid her round-trip airline ticket.

She went to the morgue and saw James sewn together. He had been hacked to pieces.

Shona demanded to see the crime scene and the police reluctantly agreed. He was murdered in the 6th floor artist studio he sublet at 737 Canal Street in Stamford. Blood was spattered on the walls. His large paper cutter was broken. The blade was the instrument of death. She sat there in that energy to make sense of what happened in a way the police could not.

The police knew who did it (officially their prime suspect). He was James' heroin dealer and had fled the country that night. Shona learned from the autopsy that James had evidence of heroin in his bones from age 12 when he was at Stowe School.

Shona paid for a party for his friends. He was, by all their accounts, a kind and gentle and generous person. There was a Mass for him at Sacred Heart Church. She then flew home with his ashes. In the summer of 1996, Serena scattered them at Ben Nevis, the highest mountain in Scotland.

James had once knocked on Shona's bedroom window in the dead of night. He had a dirk penetrating and exiting the surface of his chest. He said he could not go to the police or to a hospital. She removed it and placed her hands on the wounds. They closed up and stopped bleeding. Then they had a long talk. James told her not to worry, that he had come to this earth to explore the dark side. Shona started to understand the concept of a dualistic universe seeking balance.

How did Shona endure so much sorrow in her life and prevail over it all? She came to know her destiny. That, she believed, was the gift of James' death. She embraced the knowledge that she, in this life, was to experience the range of human experience from horror and hopelessness to sublime creative beauty and the greatest prize of all, the wisdom of truth and the wonder of love. She was here to be the villain, the hero, the queen, the warrior, the magician, the lover, the god of all, the director, all of the archetype roles in the great play on the stage of the universe.

Shona began speaking to Mothers of Murdered Children, but their grief was seeking a common solace and Shona had a different message, so she yielded her truth to theirs, as her life came into perfect focus.

Serena Bellew

Shona's only daughter, Serena Georgia Bellew, was born in London on November 13, 1969. In the hospital in St. John's Wood, Shona's room was next to Mia Farrow's and her baby.

Shona once told me a story about her daughter. I believe it was Serena's first day of school while living in Paris. A young priest was the teacher. He held up an apple and asked the class, "What is inside this apple?"

Serena Bellew | December 2005

Enthusiastic Serena knew the answer and up went her hand. He called on her. Serena said, "A star!"

"No, that's silly. Anyone else?" Serena persisted and said she was right. The priest told her to be quiet, so she sat down, embarrassed, and bewildered.

When Serena saw her mother and told her what happened, Shona went on a mission from God to that man of God. With an apple in her purse, Shona met with the priest and demanded an apology. He was completely confused by this powerful mother.

Shona sat the apple on his desk and cut it in half horizontally. Then she showed him the star inside. The inexperienced priest was incredulous and began apologizing over and over, but the damage had been done. Shona told me that Serena never again asked a question in class, all the way through her schooling, including graduate school.

When Serena was two, Richard and Shona lived for a time in Paris. Then, in 1978, Richard was transferred by I.B.M. from Paris to Connecticut where the Bellew family lived for eight years. They returned to England in 1986.

Like her younger siblings, Serena struggled academically upon returning to the U.K. As Shona writes:

> *My daughter could not adapt to the British education system, as she was very dyslexic, too. So, she returned to Connecticut and lived with friends so she could complete her last year at Greenwich High School in 1978 and graduate. She then went to the University of Wyoming. Even after returning to live in London, she continued her American education at the American College of London where she graduated with honors.*

If I remember correctly, I first met Serena when Shona took me to the re-enactment of the Battle of Jonesboro, a Civil War battle south of Atlanta that, coincidentally, involved the 63rd Georgia Volunteer Infantry Regiment of my great-grandfather. After the re-enactment Shona introduced me to her daughter.

Serena & Shona

Serena was in the uniform of a Union soldier. She was playing the authentic part of a wife disguised as a man so she could fight alongside her husband. Serena, I learned, was a serious student of history. The day we were introduced Serena had black cork on her cheeks. This was her first re-enactment and the cork represented her initiation.

After our meeting, I wrote Serena a poem about it. It was then that I learned that Serena trusted me. She said she didn't like poetry and, to this day, I don't think she has ever read it. We have had an honest relationship ever since and she knows to ask me if she ever is in need.

Fred Bellew

Henry Edward Courtenay Bellew, called "Fred," was born in London on December 14, 1973. Upon returning to England after eight years in America, Fred also found British schools challenging.

Fred, Adin & Serena

He tried for a year in the English system and eventually attended a private high school in Santa Fe, New Mexico, graduating in 1991.

I met Fred and his new bride, Melody, at his wedding in Las Vegas. Shona and I later visited the newlyweds at their home in Los Angeles and got to know them. Fred has his own computer business and is an avid gamer. I learned that Fred does a hilarious imitation of a drunk Scotsman.

Adin Bellew

Adin Nicolai Justin Patrick Bellew was born on April 7, 1980 in Greenwich, Connecticut. Shona was 40. Giving birth at her age scandalized Lady Bellew.

After her divorce from Richard, Shona moved to Rochester and lived there with her youngest son. She returned there for the remaining months of 1992 before moving to the Delphi University campus in Georgia with Adin, now fourteen, so that he could complete that semester at school. Her concern for her son's learning difficulties and her devotion to him is related in her history of his education:

> *I thought about Adin, and why I had taken all the trouble to come back here by myself as a single parent. It had been very difficult. Adin was a very happy child growing up in Connecticut. He did not appear to be dyslexic, nor have any trouble with his kindergarten lessons. My then husband worked for I.B.M. and we were always being moved. So, in 1986 we had to return to the U.K. Adin was distraught. The school he attended, The Mead School in Greenwich, Connecticut, advised us to reconsider taking him out of the country. My husband's job could not be re-negotiated, so we left the U.S.*
>
> *The problem of Adin's schooling went from bad to worse. Having lived in the U.S. for nine years, and previously for two years, we were no longer able to fit into the English way of living. Adin has always seen himself as an American and was badly teased in England for speaking in an ugly way and for being stupid. In virtually all the schools in the U.K., dyslexia is considered a form of laziness to be punished.*
>
> *He became more and more introverted and miserable until eventually I realized that if he was going to grow up in a healthy and drug free way, I would have to return him to his home, America. Professional authorities told me that he would be far better off living in the U.S. where he would grow up being properly educated.*
>
> *This has indeed proved true. The school in Rochester, New York was only for learning disabled children, and in the time he*

was there, he began to be more emotionally stable, to learn to read and write, and to develop his self-esteem again. He worked hard and began to socialize more easily.

Almost three years later, I transferred him to a school in North Carolina, The Arthur Morgan School. He has continued to overcome his learning disabilities, although he will need help throughout high school if he is to graduate and go on to college.

He has already been accepted in a private high school, Horizons, in Atlanta, that specializes in small classes and learning difficulties. He will also be attending a May audition at the North Fulton High School for the Performing Arts for their magnet program, so he has been accepted at both high schools.

For this summer, he has also been accepted by the North Carolina School of the Arts for six weeks of intensive study in the arts, a course limited to only a few exceptionally talented students.

He desperately needs to continue his education here in the U.S. He has come so far that it would be disastrous for him to leave now. He has conquered so much, but still has much left to learn about how to operate as a standard pupil in a high school and college. He is a good student and has great potential in having a successful future in business or in the arts.

I met Adin soon after Serena. He had asked Shona if he could buy a gun. Ever wise, Shona offered Adin a deal. If he would give up the idea of owning a gun, she would fund the hobby of paintball. Adin went for paintball. He joined a team as the youngest member and took me to play paintball with him. His team went to the U.S. championships and did well.

Adin was Sage's best buddy. The three of us went fishing often in the Chattahoochee River and Sage went swimming after sticks we threw.

Adin was headed to Australia for his senior year in high school as an exchange student. Shona and I took him to the airport. We told him goodbye and as he walked away, he turned and said, "If you guys want to get married, that's okay with me." We were speechless. The next time we saw Adin was at his brother's wedding in Las Vegas.

While Shona and I were in art school at Portfolio Center, Adin allowed me to use him as a model for some of my assignments. One photo of him became an award-winning book cover. But my favorite photo of him was a portrait assignment. I had his hair and skin painted using an idea from the artist René Magritte.

I guess I had some influence with Adin as he learned of my short career flying in the U.S. Air Force. General Sir Henry Leask offered to secure for Adin a commission in the Scots Guards, but Adin decided to enlist in the U.S. Air Force and did three combat tours in Iraq. I know what war does to all men. I worry about him and feel responsible.

Adin Bellew

Shona had to keep telling me another universal truth she knew, "Jay, there are no mistakes; there is only learning." One of the great privileges of loving Shona is knowing her children. I prize my close relationships with all of them.

And Shona returned those relationships to me. She was very close to my daughter and son and to all of my grandchildren. They will never forget her.

My daughter, Camilla, wrote these words about Shona:

My urge is to stay silent because how can I possibly convey the impact Shona's presence and being have had on my life? It has been a little over a year and the grief I have trickles like a stream and may become a waterfall of tears and deep sadness at any time. I write a few words here perhaps to acknowledge the loss of a true friend and mentor.

Shona brought to me a gift that few women get given from other women: the gift of seeing what it looks like when a person lives their truth authentically as best they can. That is both a process of becoming and a journey of steadfastness to be human while knowing that the only one who will truly understand this is oneself.

To me, the real story of Shona does not hinge on her abundance of experiences and adventurous accomplishments. These are but a part of her story. Shona showed me that the way of the extraordinary is accessible to everyone. She listened to her inner wisdom and acted on it, even when it did not make sense to anyone else. She showed me what a life could look like when it is lived in awareness and in connection to self.

When I compared her way of living to those of others, I saw that she did not have wealth and was still wrestling with her own inner demons. Yet she was a peaceful, contented, vibrant woman. She lived her life on her own terms ANYWAY and that was a revelation! She showed me a path to freedom and happiness that I hadn't applied to myself before.

Shona gave herself permission to allow love to be fully given and fully received, for she had a deep sense of happiness and purpose about her. In her presence, I saw a way to live that I wanted, with a freedom from outer demands and stories that keep each of us from living life as our authentic selves.

Shona had the brazen audacity to look at her dysfunctional childhood patterns and their effect on her sense of self-worth. Then she took on the arduous journey of deconstructing them and deciding to live her truth as best she could every day. She showed me how to consider other ways of thinking and interacting with the world that were kind and loving to my inner being, rather than harsh and judgmental. She taught me to forgive myself and in doing so, forgive everyone and everything else, as well.

Because of Shona, I am a more loving person and I can see a life where I live as my authentic self, a freedom that cannot be bought. Here is the thing, though. She was not any more extraordinary than any one of us. She would say that, for sure. She still had a lot of issues to deal with. She was human. She just decided to take the courageous leap of living her life in a different way, loving herself, and removing the blockages that all of us have to our own true wonderfulness.

Thank you, Shona.

Chapter Six

Our Courtship

Friends first forever,
to creative endeavor,
Spirit wove branches in part
revealing a picture,
exceedingly richer
than either had known in the heart.

Meeting Shona was like being struck a second time by lightning. She soon taught me that the universe is intentioned and that there are no accidents, so our meeting was really by destiny.

Three months after we met, Shona wrote "I think we will journey together for the rest of our lives. I only became your friend over the four days at New Year's."

Our relationship blossomed to full flower in 1998. In May she wrote, "I am really beginning to feel true safety in your arms, and in being around you, a new experience for me."

I asked her if she would agree to some boudoir photography, a private way for me to remember her in Virginia while she lived in Georgia. I explained my motive and she was thrilled. Shona wanted some clean photographs of her innocent loveliness.

I found Suna Lee in McLean, Virginia. This award-winning photographer, taught by Ansel Adams and others, had the right energy. We spent almost a day in her studio. Shona brought up a selection of clothes from Georgia. I foolishly assumed I would observe the photo shoot, but it was only Shona and Suna.

We had many favorites, but here is one of mine in my shirt, followed by one of hers.

Shona | 1998
© Suna Lee Photography

The photographs were beautiful and elegant with the spiritual energy we had hoped for. Shona treasured those photographs for the rest of her life. She told me that they made her feel honored and validated as a woman.

Einstein says the only immutable thing in the universe is the speed of light in a vacuum. Big Al is wrong. I say the *only* eternal thing in the universe is the energy of the universe, and that energy is love. It transcends time and space. I know in my heart it is the only thing that holds our universe together. What else could it be? Perhaps that is why humankind does not understand and cannot measure gravity, only see its effects, perhaps because love is misnamed gravity, the thing that attracts us together.

Shona & Big Al
March 1998

I was beginning to understand what Big Al did not. My analytical self, trained in physics and navigation, started finding balance with my intuitive, spiritual self. Our time together was turning into a glorious adventure of self-discovery, both hers and mine. By November, Shona would write, "We will love and change together as long as it makes our hearts sing, and boy does it make my heart sing!"

Shona was highly spiritual, but she was also marvelously human. Shona's favorite expletive was her made-up word: *fuckshit!* That only endeared her more to me as a powerful, truth-telling goddess. Shona was my creative and spiritual muse and, in return, let me be her warrior champion, the first she ever had. I told her I was falling in love with her. She replied, "Love is not a falling, nor is it an uplifting. Love just is!"

Shona & Jay
October 1998
Unknown Photographer

Shona & Jay
Photo by the Muppet "Grover"
during the July 4, 1998 parade in Washington, DC

When I had known Shona nine months, she wrote me this poem:

Beloved Jay

Hold my hand, and softly walk with me.
Allow my love to fold away the past.
And laugh into my eyes, Oh! man of light.
Somewhere in your heart you know
That you and I are meant to be
One and indivisible. Holy and earthly
Our love shines out, enveloping all those
Who pass us by. Feel it surging
Unchained and free, our hands held in joy,
Our hearts trembling, alive with love and passion bold.
I love you, lover, friend, confidante.
I love the strength, and the power
Of your body as it melts into mine with such
Delights that I know not where I end
And your delicious being begins.
Lips take me to the edge of time
With promises of a journey of utter bliss
Far away from the past,
From all that is not sacred, not blessed,
Into the dazzling light of the truth of you and me.

I dreamt so much of you, beloved man,
For I have known you since first I breathed.
My heart has held a vision of pure truth
Locked deeply within my breast, afraid to see,
Afraid to search for what I knew to be the real me.
You saw me first, for my eyes were blind,
And with such sweet words and looks
That I was relentlessly captured and my soul bared.
I could not resist your love, for I saw in one moment
All that I had longed for, hoped for, and believed in.

Throughout our courtship and our marriage, I was to write many songs and over 300 poems dedicated to her that I collected in a book titled *Shona, You.* This one was very meaningful to both of us.

The Dance of My Lifetime

I am dancing with you; this is the dance of my lifetime.
It is the most exciting dance of all; it is our dance, too.
This is the time I find the holiness in me;
God directs my moves.
Hopes of a lifetime dance with me
and I do not feel you in my arms.
Are you with me, darling?
No matter what, I will keep on dancing,
and you, you watch and wait.
I wondered what you were waiting for;
I wondered why.
In my waiting and wondering,
I remembered the words
God gave me for you:
I will be truly complete at dancing
when I have also learned to love waiting to dance—when I
cast aside time, cast it all.
I keep dancing; in my mind, I dance with you.
In my mind, I know I am to dance with you.
You see, I was born to dance, and I was born
to dance with you.
I will keep on dancing;
I will dance until the shoes
burn off my feet.
The world will know I have danced;
being in the world, you will know, too.
There is no more beautiful dance than this one
God has chosen for me, so, I dance in equal joy
with or without you, as you choose.
As I dance, you wait for the gold and pink sunrise,
so beautiful.
Did you know that the sunrise can be more beautiful
and more lovely for you when dancing?
Your sunrise will come and go over and over
each turn we dance, for that is what our love really is: to dance
in the glory of endless sunrises.

When you dance with me,
you will see much more
and you will hear your angel melody—
sensations for your completion.
And we will know the meaning of our lives:
to feel what the True Conductor intends.
I know I am God's beautiful instrument
and know you manifest His soul,
and we will dance until the music ends.
Still, I dance and hold out one hand to you as my heart,
so you can be part of this sacred dancing.

Shortly after we met, Shona told me she had two birthdays, one date on an Indian birth certificate, another on a British birth certificate. An avid genealogist at the time, I took up the challenge and eventually verified her true birth date of April 4, 1941 from a telegram sent by her mother to Deirdre's parents. Yes, I was in love with an older woman, and she would not tell others her age, as women often do. Besides, she looked much younger, was still fertile on her 57th birthday, and had been dating men 30 years younger before we met.

I soon discovered that she had never had a proper birthday party. Her mother had thrown one for her as a teenager, but when a boy came up and kissed Shona, Deirdre slapped Shona in the face, called her a slut with bedroom eyes, then sent everyone home.

I resolved to give her a real birthday party, even though I was in Virginia and she was living in Georgia. I sent money to a good friend of hers, Soma, with instructions.

Somehow, I learned of a talented guitarist and one-man band named Marvin Taylor who did party gigs as Five Feathers. I hired him. He was also part of the band Java Monkey. Marvin had an incredible presence. He had pure white billowing hair that flowed down, framing him like a radiant being. And he had a kindness to match.

Shona insisted I wear my Air Force dress uniform from my active duty days while she wore my flight suit with flowers in her hair.

Shona had indeed reinvented herself—she was no longer the conventional aristocrat. Her eclectic friends came, and I met some interesting new people. I could see they adored her.

Shona on Her 57th Birthday

Marvin Taylor & Jay Harden
Unknown Photographer

A few days later we went to hear Java Monkey play at Fuzzy's Place in Atlanta, not far away from Dunwoody. The band was so deafening that we could not hear the tornado outside. We left and were stopped short of her home by a police barricade. Against their advice, we walked in on foot, stepping over live power lines, and checked on her daughter, Serena (who was away at a friend's and safe), and Sage, that wonder dog who had been present when we first met.

Shona, Sage, and I stayed overnight in a local La Quinta Inn that still had electrical power. By destiny, we had to share our first bed together and there we first made love. Sage will swear to it.

Now I should relate the amazing story of Sage. Sage was selected as a puppy for his high intelligence, then trained to be a service dog for a young girl of 14 with a severe disability. Sadly, she died at the time Sage completed his training with her. Sage could not be retrained for another person, so Shona got him for the cost of his shots and papers.

I was slowly discovering Shona's spiritual power to attract good things into her life. She took Sage for daily walks on wooded trails. He was a free spirit just like her. People they passed often commented on the sheen of his coat and mistook him for a much younger dog. And Sage did not smell like a dog at all. I knew the smell of a dog and he didn't have it.

Once day I was in her kitchen and noticed a wonderful aroma coming from the stewpot. Shona's roommate, Sherry Wheat, told me not to touch it. Why not? Because it was for Sage. Yes, that's right. Shona cooked for Sage. He loved Shona's stew of vegetables and boneless chicken breasts, supplemented with raw bones she got from a butcher to satisfy his need for chewing and to clean his teeth. Her menu was the secret of his lustrous coat and huggable smell.

Sage was intuitive like Shona. He sensed my emotional state and knew when I needed him before I did. Whenever a bout of depression hit me, Sage would come around and not leave me alone. I had to deal with him and play, so he forced me through my depression. Sage was Shona's dog, he was Adin's dog, he was our dog, and he was mine. Sage saved my life, literally and emotionally. That enlightened dog blessed my life. God, how I miss him, too.

Jay, Adin & Sage
© Shona Harden

Sage and Adin and I went fishing together often. Sage loved to retrieve sticks from the water. His energy was infectious. After he shook himself dry, he did not even smell like the Chattahoochee River.

One day on his walk, Shona met Eric Peters and his older female Black Labrador. Those dogs fell in love with each other. It was an amazing thing to see them in such joyous play. Eric told Shona that if she ever parted with Sage, he would take him. Of course, she said, "Never."

During the Blizzard of 1999, the three of us were living in Northern Virginia. One snowy night, I had my first heart attack. They called for a helicopter, but it was grounded by ice. I remember the snow falling on my face as EMS took me to the hospital. Shona could not go with me because we were not married at the time, so she commandeered a neighbor to take her to the hospital and beat us there.

I recovered, but we realized that the energy of Washington was lethal and decided to leave that unfeeling place. Shona wanted to return to Atlanta where her daughter, Serena, was in graduate school. My amazing love traveled down to Georgia and found us a rental house, then organized everything and moved us. I was unable to lift a thing. She told me the landlord did not allow pets, so she contacted Eric and gave up Sage because of me.

According to Eric, Sage had a wonderful life. He sent us pictures and Sage looked happy, but fat. He did not maintain Shona's diet. Eric told us when Sage died of old age. I still feel guilty and responsible for the loss of Sage. I loved that dog more than any other animal in my life. He was another happy version of Shona.

At some point, my inner wisdom told me to do something, so I did. I went to a jewelry store in Tyson's Corner, Virginia and bought a gold band 8mm wide. I had it engraved on the outside to read SHONA WAS CREATED TO BE TREASURED. This was a truth about her that had never been said or written down. Now the truth of Shona was made permanent to remind her and all who saw it.

I decided it was time for Shona to meet my daughter and her family, so I drove us to St. Louis. On the way I told her what spirit had instructed me to do. I gave the ring to her. I made it clear that although it looked like a wedding band, it was not. I was merely the messenger and the sender was spirit, not me.

Shona was incredulous, beaming with joy. That little girl of hers was validated by the universe. It was a wonderful moment for us both. When she put it on, my mission was complete.

Later, while we were in school together at Portfolio Center, I did an assignment with my view camera that showed her ring alongside the inner workings of my grandfather's pocket watch.

Shona loved jewelry and she wore that ring on and off the rest of her life, so much that the engraving has worn down. She was wearing it when she died and her daughter, Serena, returned it to me later. Now I wear it on my little finger, my secret satisfaction. It fits perfectly.

Chapter Seven

Shona, Spirituality & Healing

She brings to all and me
a spirituality:
a joy so free and pure,
from light that will endure.

It took many years and many further traumas in Shona's life before she could liberate herself from the suffocation of English conventions, but she then began to understand that famous quote attributed to Mark Twain, "The two most important days in your life are the day you were born and the day you find out why." Our adventures with healing our souls were about to begin.

By the time I met Shona, she had been on a long journey to try to heal the deep traumas and abuses that she had experienced. My road, on the other hand, was just beginning. Neither of us had any idea that day how much we had in common—or that our childhood wounds would lead us to an amazing 33 years of life-long friendship and marriage.

Shona's earliest step as a healer was an unintended gift from her daughter Serena, then about five years old. When Serena started slowly losing her hearing, Shona took conventional advice and sought the best, most expensive doctors and their treatments, with no success. Shona was told that her daughter was going to be deaf for the rest of her life, but Shona refused to accept it In desperation, she turned to a free homeopathic hospital avoided by the aristocracy.

While examining Serena, the doctor asked Shona if her daughter had a recent concussion or fall on the head. Shona said no, but bright Serena spoke up. "Yes, Mum, don't you remember when I fell out of the park swing onto the concrete?" That was the crucial bit of information.

The doctor compounded a powder with a mortar and pestle and over time Serena's hearing slowly returned. Her hearing is still perfect today. Experiencing this changed Shona's view of conventional medicine forever. She kept her children free of inoculations when she became an ordained minister and Shona herself never took any prescription medication until her final illness.

Her daughter's healing was a turning point in Shona's life that cascaded into a turning point in my own life and in other clients and friends who were guided to Shona for spiritual and physical help. Through the years, she sought further training and became certified as a practitioner in an amazing array of modalities from Bach Flower Essences to Deep Tissue Massage, Shiatsu, Rebirthing, RoHun Therapy™, and Spiritual Counseling.

In her search to educate herself, Shona developed a vast knowledge of the world's ley lines by visiting sacred areas in Britain and Egypt. For twelve years she guided others on tours of these sites. She studied ancient manuscripts and comparative religions and trained in Bioenergetics, Macrobiotics, Meditation, Inner Child, Loving Relationship Training, and Gestalt Therapy, to name a few. In 1993, she became an ordained minister in the Church of Wisdom. The certifying body was Delphi University. She also practiced as a Parapsychology Counselor and as a Medium.

In 1981 Shona was diagnosed as having breast cancer. As she later wrote while we were married:

Back then there were minimal medical solutions, and little was really known on how to cure it. Chemo was pronounced as the best solution so far, and various other drugs were coming on the market. I was very blessed to come across a very crass and unsympathetic doctor. It was the end of a long hospital day. Tired and stressed, he told me that I had breast cancer in my left breast. It had been clearly picked up by my recent mammogram test. He told me not to worry, that if worse came to worse, I would have one removed, but that I had another one which showed no sign of cancer, so far.

Sadly, he did not know that I was very involved in the La Leche League promoting breast feeding and a healthy respect for the female body, particularly the breasts. I was horrified and fled, deciding that, as I had already lived a long and full life, I could die in dignity. Besides, I had already left this world on board ship travelling from Bombay to Cape Town when I was a toddler. I contracted scurvy, became very ill, and died. I was happy to leave—I had had an awful childhood to that point, so I was very glad to die.

But life, God/Goddess, All That Is, had other plans. I was turned down and told to return as it was not my time to die yet. Despairing and angry, I had no choice then, but perhaps this time I would make it, I would have a choice.

For about three weeks I vacillated between the two possibilities. An introduction to an alternative healing center in Massachusetts and a young, phenomenally wise therapist made the decision for me, and my journey to health and wholeness began.

Shona told me she refused conventional treatment. As she had already worked so extensively in the alternative healing modalities, she decided to heal herself with the help of the therapist she had met, a macrobiotic diet, Alexander Lowen's Bioenergetics, the work of Louise Hay, and a great deal of spiritual unfoldment.

One of the things her inner wisdom told her was to scream away that toxic energy. She taught herself to do what she had never dared before. She spent months driving around the nearby roads with the radio turned up and allowing a lifetime of rage to erupt into the air, along with tears. When the weather was bad, she just sat in her car in the garage and did the same. Her solution made so much sense to me.

Two years later, when she returned to the doctor who did the original mammogram, he did another to see if the tumor had grown. He checked and rechecked them against each other. Then he finally admitted to Shona that he could find no evidence of any lump at all, benign or malignant.

Having learned a great deal firsthand about illness, its causes, and its cures, Shona began public speaking and teaching. One workshop she developed was called *Heal Thyself* which encouraged women to take responsibility for their own health and well-being. She continued her healing practice in massage, alternative health, and offering dietary advice. She developed a service called *Alternatives* to help the general public find out information about alternative therapies, events, and technologies available at that time. Sometimes using radio, but mostly being invited to speak at meetings and luncheons, Shona met and inspired many people until the very end of her life.

In September of 2004, I put into the following words my understanding of Shona's healing work.

> *When people ask me what my wife does, I tell them she is a spiritual counselor. "And what," they ask, "is that?" This is the point where it becomes a little difficult for me, for there is no simple explanation.*
>
> *Instead, I describe for them a mythical counseling client of hers, a representative archetype. This person is just as likely to be a woman or a man, say someone from his late twenties through the fifties. He is seeking some answer to a life situation and has been at it unsuccessfully for some time.*
>
> *To him life is and remains a beguiling mystery. We humans, it seems, are the only living beings for which this is true. We are the only ones who seek beyond mere survival. Because the moon hangs in the sky we wonder why it does and what it is like there. It is our very nature to seek. We seek because we want to find, to puzzle out, to know the secrets of everything.*

This typical client of my wife's has done most, if not all, the things expected of him by the world and by himself. He has his own independent family. He provides. He plays. He eats his vegetables and he goes to church. He has a good job, a house, and his toys. By any outward measure he is a success. He has grown in competence by making mistakes. He is responsible and plans for tomorrow. He is respected and he is loved.

And yet this man does not feel complete. He is aware he is restive for no apparent reason. Everything he has tried has soothed only in a fleeting way. He is in the world but does not feel fully a part of it. For all his effort to direct and control his own life, he remains at the effect of the seeming random universe. External forces, usually a powerful blow from life like a severe and inexplicable personal loss, drive him toward this counseling.

This is the kind of person who comes to talk to my wife: someone very much like you and me—a real person with honest questions.

Inevitably, the first question he asks is: "What is wrong?" And her reassuring answer is always: "Nothing is wrong. You are on a path to find your own happiness and right now that path has led you here." Although each client has a unique healing path from suffering to happiness, generally the process starts with identifying negative stories from the client's past (even concerns about the future prove to be based on past stories) that create judgment and suffering.

Now the word happiness may be misleading. We are biologically programmed in our cells and DNA to seek. First, we seek survival, then security, then society. Finally, we seek who we really are, who we were uniquely created to be. Instead of happiness, some call this God, some call it inner peace, some call it source, union, or our ultimate unboundedness. By whatever name, we want it.

This motivating force is true for all of us, newborn to ancient, high to low, without exception. It may be easy to imagine this is true of Buddha or the Christ, but not so easy to image for Bin Laden or Charles Manson. Yet, it is so. Each of us is compelled by birthright to seek this, the greatest prize of living.

Finally, intuition, frustration, or recommendation leads this man or woman to become a client seeking spiritual counseling. Every complaint of every client can be traced inevitably back to that primal longing to know oneself.

After assurance, Shona then acknowledges the courage that brought him here, for his path toward self-realization, though timeless, is not yet in the mainstream of America healing. She tells him her model of spiritual counseling evolves from a few fundamental truths.

Shona used these truths to guide many others toward profound self-healing. In her methodology, the client is the doer and she is only the facilitator. As she told me:

> *First, the thing that all humans seek, happiness or whatever you call it, can only be found within. Some of us try to find this through alcohol, drugs, violence, sex, religion, relationships, or countless other addictive behaviors. These cannot succeed for the simple reason that they exist outside ourselves. The transitory peace they may bring is in them, not created and carried within us. Everything external is transitory by nature and therefore beyond our real control—both joys and sorrows—a human theory of relativity through direct experience.*
>
> *Happiness exists in the present moment, and only in the present moment. Therefore, living in the present moment is the only way to find the happiness you seek. In other words, it is impossible to be unhappy in the present. Awareness will tell you always where you live. Whenever you realize you are not happy, know you are not in the present: you are living either in the past or the future.*
>
> *The client's work then consists of learning how to live constantly in the present, to stop living in the emotions of the past and the concerns of the future, both forms of suffering.*
>
> *Suffering is another name for unhappiness. Suffering is not our natural condition. We are born with certain emotions: happiness, sadness, anger, and fear. But every other feeling is learned: shame, blame, guilt, loss, sin, criticism, etc. We are not born sufferers: yet, this is what we learn. We are born happy and gradually lose it through faulty learning. The older we get, the more vigorously we seek happiness and the less we find.*
>
> *The second great truth is that all suffering is a result of personal judgment. Whenever we judge others, we create suffering*

for ourselves. It eventually becomes clear that all outer judgment is, in fact, disguised self-judgment. This is an inevitable and breakthrough realization as the client validates this truth by examination of his own experience.

Finally, the client comes to know that, since judgment is a self-created illusion, there are no mistakes in life, only learning, and that they can trust themselves in all things. They can faithfully depend upon themselves and have no need of outside structures to guide or control their life.

Shona had infinite empathy for the struggles of others and deep wisdom to convey to us about love and relationships.

Her own words expressed this best.

You will see that there are underlying principles which, when truly understood, will give you a foundation of safety and security with yourself and your world. The reason the security with yourself is so important is that safety has nothing to do with an event or situation.

For some people, the idea of mountain climbing would be terrifying. Without the acquired knowledge and skills, you could not trust yourself to not fall. Another person, however, with the appropriate skills would consider climbing a grand and very exciting adventure. The situation is the same, the difference is simply the trust and confidence that the skilled person had in their ability to climb safely, allowing the situation to become fun instead of a nightmare.

It is the same with life. Few people were given the skills and knowledge of how to live a life full of adventure, success, and prosperity, at the same time feeling safe and secure within themselves. The art of living fully will encompass awareness of all the varied levels of one's being: physical, mental, emotional, spiritual, psychic, magical, cosmic, and angelic.

Seems like a lot. It is. We are multidimensional beings, and we were created to live life that way, on many dimensions. The gift of these various levels, bodies, and dimensions is that they are interlinked. They feed each other, open doors for each other, support and bless each other.

They can give you insights into realities that open your heart, nurture your soul, and unlock your little child from his/her banishment. These doorways or if you like, pathways, will give you back the understanding of who you really are. They contain all the tools, wisdom, and knowledge you will ever need to be safe for the rest of your existence and beyond. They will allow you to wake up in the morning, day after day, with a song in your heart that can never be silenced. You will find that these tools will give you the power and the self-esteem that allow you to accomplish whatever you desire, and to always have your achievements in alignment with the highest good of all, regardless of color, creed, or nationality. You will find that you have no enemies, only great teachers.

You will only be able to live win/win lives from then on, not because that will be a goal for you, but because when you are in alignment with all that you are, you cannot live any other way. You will be expressing the Divine power of the I AM Presence that is your essence and the truth of who you are.

You came from the realms of light to explore the concept of duality here on earth, to explore two different angles of life, good and bad, to experience choice as never before, and to examine it so closely that you live with it daily. You all become actors on the stage of life, exploring more of who you all are. In this theater, you are not only the actors, but the writer of the plays, the director, and the audience. In this way you become mirrors to each other throughout the entire run of the play.

It is so very much easier to see a fault in another than in oneself, is it not? Of course! For when the issue is one step removed from you, it is always easier to see. You cannot see your face unless it is reflected back at you in some kind of reflection.

Now, when you add another ingredient to this scenario, that of love, then the mirror becomes so much more encompassing. Nothing evades the all-seeing eye of love. It is the greatest healer on the earth. In fact, it is the only energy there is on earth. Everything is love and its only nature is to love. It shines on the shadows of your pain, suffering, anger, shame, and blame, so that you can see it all and release it.

Love shines the strongest in the face of your beloved, your children, and your family. The darkest shadows will always be present there, but so is the greatest healing.

Sadly, most of the time we do not understand what is happening. We say that the shit has hit the fan when the honeymoon seems over, or when that perfect job turns sour. But this shit is the very shadow that you have brought into the relationship or into that job. It is this shadow that love now brings to the surface for you to heal so that you may be at peace again.

The deeper the love, the deeper the level of shadow that will surface, and often at an overwhelming pace. The difficulty is that most of us do not have the tools to deal with this dilemma. The shadows stay projected onto the loved ones or the work colleagues instead of being seen as gifts and a chance to clear hidden pain from within ourselves and create happiness. If we cannot see these shadows in ourselves or from our past, and we believe instead that it is the other person doing it to us, then the only alternative is to criticize or condemn the other person, or to walk away, losing a wonderful opportunity for growth, and usually leaving unfinished business behind.

So, little by little, the breakdown of the relationship begins, until there is separation, blame, anger, and pain. Then on to the next person, only this time we will make sure that they are very different than the last one. They will have different characteristics, and different habits. But the mirror of love follows you wherever you go, in relationships, business, friends, or church, for love is ever present and its nature is only to bring peace, harmony, and balance to you and your world. You will find that although partners will vary in looks, culture, habits, and characteristics, somehow pain, anger, and blame come with them anyway until the pattern is healed. Then the partner's behavior will appear to change.

There were so many things that Shona showed me and all of us about the healing powers of love.

Perhaps the greatest personal truth she taught me is now a permanent part of my consciousness. We both said this to each other, particularly at moments of difficulty when we needed a reminder:

Jay, you are an innocent man.
I adore you.
And everything else is just stuff.

Shona, you are an innocent woman.
I adore you.
And everything else is just stuff.

Our love for each other was unconditional and our stuff was just another layer of the onion coming up to be healed, something to be welcomed. Stuff is the litter of life to be embraced. In these few words, I found the formula for a happy life with her—and, now—without her. Her voice, full of forgiveness and love of me, rings in my heart every day.

I also learned from Shona that I cannot suffer in the present moment. All my suffering occurs, without exception, in the past. I cannot heal my childhood and combat traumas in the present moment. Shona guided me to go back into my past and heal it there. What a gift she gave me! I would never have figured that out by myself.

Along the way, Shona gently (and sometimes not-so-gently) led me into other intense spiritual adventures I would never have taken without her. In 1999, while Shona and I were living together in Virginia, we were guided to heal our sexual wounds from childhood and to learn the ancient arts of sacred sexual energy called *kundalini*. We already knew of the beautiful work of tantrika Margo Anand through her book, *The Art of Sexual Magic*, and her beautiful DVD showing actual tantra in practice. We also knew the book, *Jewel in the Lotus*, written by Sunyata Saraswati and Bodhi Avinasha, as well as other works.

To our luck, we found Jade Garden in nearby Olney, Maryland that taught classes in tantra. Each class of limited size had an equal number of men and women, taught by a man and female assistants. We signed up. The classes were not lectures only; they were mostly practices. We learned such things as the yab-yum position and intimate eye gazing, left eye to left eye. We were often paired randomly to a stranger of opposite gender. This required great trust, especially for me. Kundalini is a very powerful energy. After a few classes, it overwhelmed me. While Shona stayed stalwart, I reverted back to pure fear and we had to leave, forfeiting our tuition.

Before that happened, something else did. It turned out to be the real reason we were destined to go to Jade Garden.

During a break, I overheard a conversation between two students: a female psychologist and another woman. The doctor was telling her of a client who had completed an intensive weekend for men, something called New Warrior. I thought only women had intensive feminist weekends. This was new information and I was curious. So, I approached her for details. Her client had come back so transformed, so improved to his family, that his son also completed the weekend. Now, I was hooked. She gave me a scribbled piece of paper with a web site, *www.mkp.org*.

The next day I investigated and decided to attend their upcoming free introductory presentation. That night I went early to get a good seat. What I witnessed astonished me. A group of men were setting up the meeting. Something about how they interacted fascinated me. Their energy was different, so clear and clean, unlike my previous competitive connections with the military officer community and government service, and not at all like the different bond of love between brothers in combat. For the first time in my life I saw men hugging each other. Not like women who lean into each other and fake kiss on the cheek. These men hugged naturally, eye to eye with no disempowering slaps on the back, no sexual energy at all. I didn't understand what I saw, but I knew for certain that whatever they had, I wanted it for me.

I remember the two things they promised on the New Warrior Training Adventure. First, my personal safety was guaranteed. And, second, I could leave at any time, no questions asked. I returned home to Shona. We discussed New Warrior at length. She intuitively knew what the weekend was about without knowing the details. I did research for months searching for those details. No luck. Finally, it was time to decide.

Shona told me to come into the body and stand with feet apart, then anchor myself to the earth and grow roots out my feet down to the center of the earth. I did. Then she said to call into consciousness my divine inner wisdom. I did. Then she taught me to ask that wisdom any simple Yes or No question. She said I would get an instant response bypassing my conscious rational mind. I asked my divine inner wisdom: am I supposed to go on the New Warrior weekend? The instant answer was Yes.

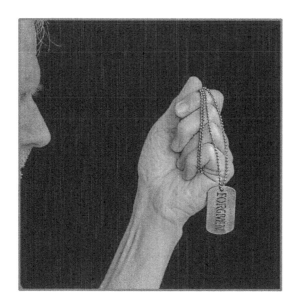

Jay in 1999
© Journey Carolyn Collins

I applied and paid my tuition of $750. No one else was allowed to pay it for me. I had to demonstrate to them and myself that I was worth the investment. And so it happened on a Friday afternoon in late August. I left for my NWTA full of abnormal fear, for obvious reasons, but bold enough from the support of my biggest believer in me, Shona.

Jay in 1999
© Unknown Photographer

I completed NWTA with a personal mission statement for the rest of my life that I still follow and carry in my wallet. I would dearly love to share here the details of that transformational weekend, but I won't ruin the experience for other new warriors to come. I will just show the two Polaroids taken of me when I showed up and when I left. At first, my New Warrior brothers call me Knowing Hawk, but I have since taken the name Fiery Songbird.

In 2003, Shona introduced me to another spiritual adventure. We both participated in a Soul Recognition workshop in North Carolina that led to a sacred reconciliation with myself. What I had never known (and I didn't know any men who had) was the unconditional love of *women*. To my eternal delight, that is what I found at Shona's urging.

The workshop consisted of myself and 17 women, being led by Flo Magdalena. These were not ordinary women, believe me—they were gorgeous, graceful goddesses all. I was, to put it kindly, disoriented. I had never seen such a group. It was their eyes. All of them were clear and intelligent, sparkling and comfortable, deep and calm.

Something else was up that is very hard to describe. A clear feeling permeated the workshop space. I can only explain it as a palpable, creative energy that held all of us together gently, a kind of unifying field that my scientific mind and vocabulary could not fully encompass. I became a part of their energy.

These women, all of them, willingly gave me their attention. They listened and heard me. They really saw me, they touched me, they laughed with me, and they honored me in my strengths and weaknesses. It was a beautiful, humbling, and sacred experience that inevitably opened a part of me long hidden from myself and the world.

Soul Recognition Workshop | 2003
Unknown Photographer

Perhaps the most profound experience I had of Shona's ability to lead me to a place of healing occurred when we visited the town of my birth together. Shona knew the intimate details of my childhood rape and near death. She alone knew of my need to get some sort of justice for my little boy, justice he never got. His only champion, me, had to do something for his great suffering so young and uncomforted.

So we drove south in our van and visited my hometown and the scene of that long-ago crime. For some reason, I felt I needed to stop at a Walmart on the way. I purchased a sledgehammer.

We drove to Old Prospect Church outside of town, but services were going on and the parking lot was full. So, we visited the decaying farmhouse nearby where my father was born a few minutes after his fraternal twin, Harmon, named for the Confederate family hero. My father never knew what his brother did to me.

We returned to the church, now empty. I was trembling. I walked to Harmon's headstone next to his parents. And I swung that sledgehammer. And I screamed and cried. I was back in time guided by my little kid. He was swinging that sledgehammer, slowly lifting that dark cloud over me I had carried since then. I was in a surreal, altered mental state, slinging snot through the air as I raged on and on.

Try as hard as I could, I was unable to shatter that six-inch thick piece of granite. An eight-pound sledgehammer was not heavy enough. I kept swinging until I was exhausted. I managed to deface his carved name. Then I got inspired and swung an upward stroke to the corner. Off came a nice shard of granite. I took that home as my trophy where it is still stored today in my footlocker.

I had hoped to be discovered in the act of vandalism. That way the police would charge me with desecrating a grave and the reporters would be there. This would be big news in that small town. Then I could testify in print to the world. Harmon's children did not want to bother with his funeral, so they donated his body to some medical school. I knew there was no body beneath that stone and the charge would have to be dropped. My final act after I calmed down was to slip a dog tag between the stone and the earth. The dog tag contained the word **FORGIVEN** cut through it.

Throughout all this, Shona held a safe space for me next to the van. She was truly my guardian angel. She gave me permission to do what I was guided to do. She completely accepted me, putting aside her own memories of abuse more horrific than mine.

Shona and I went south for the last time a few years later. We visited the grave of my first wife, Carolyn, and my son, the place where I will join them someday. Then we went back to Old Prospect Church to see if the stone had been replaced.

Surrounding the cemetery were motion-activated lights, with words to the effect that the premises were monitored 24 hours and violators would be prosecuted. I didn't check the headstone, but I did smile at the power of my little kid to change this part of the world.

Shona pronounced my healing complete. I felt no shame anymore. I was ready to tell my truth to anyone who cared to hear it. Thanks to her understanding, her patience with me, and her willingness to be present with me as a witness, I was able to get the only justice possible for that four-year-old Jay, the boy who lived. I will never be able to repay my Shona for her immense act of love.

All of these life-altering experiences happened to me simply because this disguised goddess, my wife Shona, the most powerful, lovely, loveable, and loving woman I've ever known, showed me where I needed to go. That is what our deep love had always done. In February of 2005 I took this photo of her at Hilton Head Island in our hot tub full of bubble bath. This is my best effort to wordlessly show Shona as that healer and angelic being she remains across space and time.

Shona | 2005

Chapter Eight

Shona's Many Talents

*Here is the place
we have sought for so long,
where everything necessary is possible
and love is clear for all time.*

Cosmic artist, healer, hot air balloonist, race car mechanic, baseball player, Olympic dancer, model, educator, writer . . . it seems impossible that any one person could possess so many diverse talents or experience so many adventures in one lifetime. Initially, I found it hard to believe the stories Shona casually told me, but in every case, I found them to be true.

Shona the Artist Inspiration

Early in our relationship Shona told me about Terence Cuneo. Sir George Bellew had commissioned him to do a portrait of Shona as an engagement present after his genealogy research found her of suitable blood to marry his son. I thought it was a high honor to have someone paint your portrait, something I, as a once aspiring artist, envied. Shona's story was casual and intriguing.

Terence was a renowned artist already. He painted the June 2, 1963 coronation of Queen Elizabeth II in Westminster Abbey. The massive painting took another year to complete and was about six feet high by eight feet wide and contained individual portraits of the more than 3,000 people shown, using a photograph he took at that moment. He had the 52 royals sit later to add their faces, including Sir George Bellew.

Terence was also famous for other subjects including horses, trains, and scenes of the American West. He was also noted for his portraits of famous people portrayed as mice and Richard Bellew inherited several. The accidental story of how Cuneo came to paint mice is fascinating in itself.

When Sir George saw the finished portrait of Shona, he was enraged. I have never been able to find out exactly why. Even more unbelievable, he refused to accept or even pay for the work, hardly the behavior of an aristocrat English gentleman in the Royal Household!

Shona at Age 23 | Shona at Age 57

Shona told me that her relationship while sitting with Terence became a spiritual connection. I think it is for that reason that he referred to her painting as *Portrait of a Lady* in his biography, which Cuneo insisted the title be: *The mouse & His Master*. Although he never identified her by name, he also added a note: "The commission that was never claimed and one which I could never part with." It hung over the mantle in his house.

Shona lost contact with Cuneo and at my urging tried to find him, but he had already died.

Thanks to the efforts of Richard Bellew, Shona and I were able to visit the current owner of the portrait, Terence's granddaughter, Melanie Cuneo, in 1998. The portrait positively glowed to my eyes with a living subtlety.

I used Photoshop on my photograph of the portrait to recreate the original. That photo was made with a 6-megapixel Canon D60, state of the art at the time.

My copy of Shona's portrait at age 23 now hangs in my entrance hall as another way to cherish her and make me smile inside.

Shona the Race Car Mechanic

One thing Shona loved was cars. The year was 1966 and Shona was 25 years old. As she related:

> I built a Lotus 2+2 and got an offer to work with Alain de Cadenet to be a Formula 2 racing mechanic. I started learning to strip and rebuild engines and drive a D2 Jaguar. I drove the huge transporter across the English Channel and down to Le Mans for the first time. I worked on all sorts of great cars. I drove mini-Minors and did laps [165 mph, she told me] at Targa Florio and the Nürburgring. Richard loved it because he could come into the pits at all the races.

Her ability to connect with her intuition was very valuable to the team in cutting down the time needed to identify mechanical problems during a race. Shona showed me how her hands were damaged from working on his race cars.

Alain de Cadenet drove a red Ferrari Dino and a green Ford McLaren. He knew Shona well and Shona became godmother to his daughter, Amanda, then Alain became godfather to her son, Henry (Fred).

As Alain wrote to me recently:

> I've often wondered what happened to dear Shona after she left Petersham Mews. She has been one of the few pragmatic and able women that I have ever met. She always had the amazing curiosity for just everything that passed before her eyes.
>
> I'm sure you know all about her father-in-law, very British, very proper, always with an eye on propriety and being seen to conform to acceptable behavior. Shona could do exactly what was required when needs be. But it was not her natural, vivacious way at all.
>
> Filled with an abundance of joy, intermingled with her 'can-do' philosophy, she was always determined to make the most of every day she was given. She certainly took to motor racing as an adventure that needed investigation. Wielding spanners (wrenches), rolling fat wheels with fat tyres thereupon and just being useful was her forte.
>
> Shona got along very well with my erstwhile co-driver, Chris Craft, and also my then friend John Wolfe. John was killed on the first lap of the 1969 Le Mans 24 Hour race. Devastating for us all.
>
> I am delighted to hear that you married her and did 22 years together. Exceptional ladies like Shona were rare in that period and more so today with youth overwhelmed by Apple and worse.
>
> Did she ever tell you the story about borrowing my Super 8 cine camera to film her daughter's christening in the U.S.? When she went to the local camera shop to pick up the movie; it was playing on a screen in the shop window.

Shona's love for speed led to a number of run-ins with the law. When Shona moved to McCaysville, a small town of 1,000 people, to attend Delphi University, you can bet that they never had encountered anyone like her.

Shona was constantly stopped for speeding in her red Toyota MR2 by the local police force consisting of one old man who used his own vehicle as a police car. "Now Grit Lady, you gotta stop speeding," he told her over and over again. She charmed him, of course, and never got a ticket.

Shona had acquired the nickname of "Grit Lady" when she visited the local breakfast joint. At "Kay's Kountry Kitchen" she ordered eggs from Kay herself. Kay asked Shona, "Do you want grits with that?" She had no idea what grits were, so my adventurous love responded, "I believe I'll try one." With that, the entire restaurant of male rednecks perked up and watched this lady with her strange accent.

Kay came back with her order. On her plate was a single cooked ground grain of corn. Shona said, "I must have made a mistake. What is that?" Then the entire restaurant erupted in laughter. Shona smiled as Kay explained. And from that day Shona became known locally as "Grit Lady."

Shona & Her Red Toyota MR2

When I first met Shona, she was still driving her red Toyota MR2. She picked me up at the Atlanta Airport and sped us away. She also used that tiny speedster to tow her 16 foot boat, or rather it seemed the boat towed her. That was some sight! Once we hauled a full-sized refrigerator on the back. She simply would not yield to my conventional advice. Others looked and shook their heads. Me, I smiled. What man would not want a beautiful woman by his side flying down the road in a red car with the wind in his face listening to great music? And aviator sunglasses. Some dreams do come true.

Next she had a 2002 torch red Mustang GT convertible with black flames down the side. It was impeccable and in Georgia Bulldogs colors, too. I was not allowed to drive it because the transmission was, as she put it, "too tight."

Shona was a masterful, confident driver. I trusted her at any speed. One day she told me about driving the back roads of England using her knees to steer while she did her knitting. At that point in our relationship nothing surprised me about living and loving and surrendering to a goddess.

Shona loved cars like I loved airplanes and we went to many airshows taking biplane rides and photographs, but Shona was also a fellow aviator at heart.

She would often speak a thought aloud and say, "This is a beautiful day." And I always replied, "Yes, you are." It never failed to produce her accepting smile. And a silent satisfaction for me.

Shona the Aviator

The day I met Shona, she told me in a matter-of-fact manner that she was a hot air balloon pilot, one of the first women in England to get her license. She didn't know then that I had been on a B-52 crew in Vietnam. I found it hard to believe her, but I said nothing, only inquired about her logbook. She said she still had it somewhere.

As our relationship bloomed to friendship, she told me more. She started flying when she was living in Paris on Avenue Kléber.

She learned at Malcom Forbes' place at Baleroi in Normandy. Shona first flew on June 16, 1978 under the instruction of John R. Gore, then soloed in September, flying from Ecchinshall to Watership Down.

On her check ride, Shona crashed the balloon and there was a fire. Her instructor was so impressed by Shona's handling of the emergency that he passed her anyway and she got her license on October 5, 1978. She told me she once landed unintentionally in a restricted area and was immediately surrounded by law enforcement. As usual, she charmed her way out of that.

Richard bought her a Colting 77 balloon named Hombre (registration EIBFG). He eventually tired of chasing her in his car and being her ground crew. Her flying career ended when he sold the balloon without her knowledge. Her log shows her last flight was on June 7, 1979 with a career total of 49 hours and 30 minutes of flying time.

Shona flew for The Mead School in Greenwich, Connecticut and in the Great Pumpkin Balloon Rally in Newton, Massachusetts in October 1978. In November of that year, she flew in Albuquerque. She also flew commercially for National Westminster Bank, New York. I know all this is true because she eventually found her logbook. I still have it.

Shona the Egyptian Tour Guide

Egypt was another spiritual adventure for my future life partner.

After I.B.M. transferred Richard and Shona back to the U.K. a second time, Shona continued her independent ways. In 1986, she led a guided tour of Egypt in unconventional style. Her group stayed with locals, not in commercial hotels, and travelled the Nile in traditional felucca sailboats.

Shona sailed the group down the Nile to Hatshepsut's Temple and Luxor near the Valley of the Kings, and to the Temple of Isis at Philae on Agilkia Island.

One night she went alone to one of the pyramids, bribed a guard, and climbed to the top, scarring her shins. The capstone was missing, of course. As she laid on her back with arms outstretched, unable to see any of the pyramid, she felt the sensation of floating in the heavens.

She managed to get down before dawn undetected and wrote this poem on her birthday as "a present to me."

> *I am a bird of the Nile,*
> *I swim in her waters,*
> *I fly in the air on wings of the wind.*
> *I choose the currents of life's highways.*
> *I am free; free to experience, to discover all of me.*

Shona the Baseball Player

Not long after I met her, Shona told me another of her matter-of-fact hard-to-believe stories.

It all began in 1994. She was in Sedona, Arizona selling posters at a Dali Lama conference and chatting with John Taylor, a baseball coach from Boston. Oh, that's nice, she told him, I never heard of baseball.

They became close friends and hiked the local canyons. He said he had two tickets to a minor league game behind home plate. By habit, he brought his glove, then let her wear it. Shona stuck up her arm and caught a foul ball. He exclaimed, "I've been to over 500 games and I've never caught a ball!" The fans around them cheered her and Shona became infatuated with baseball. John gave her a bat and glove and taught her to hit, catch, and throw in Boynton Canyon. She asked if she could play baseball. "No women," he replied. And they went their separate ways.

Somehow Shona managed to talk herself onto a men's baseball team back in Dunwoody, Georgia. They needed a catcher. She was the only woman in the league.

Shona in Catcher's Gear
Unknown Photographer

A short time later, she was at a party and went up to a young man, introduced herself, and asked him, "What do you do?" He said that he was unemployed. Undeterred as usual, she tried to recruit him for her baseball team. Amused, he said nothing, then revealed that he played for the Atlanta Braves and they were on strike. He was enthralled by Shona and remarked that he hadn't been as enthusiastic as her since he was nine years old and noticed by baseball scouts.

Shona hired a former coach of the Braves to teach her how to hit at the local batting cages. He saw her focused intent and shared with her some of the secret rules of baseball he had learned over his career. One was a revelation to her that she applied to her life and taught her therapy clients: 'You will never be successful until you learn to enjoy the waiting." Shona continued catching for her team until she was injured.

Her story was still hard for naïve me to grasp. My lovely lady pulled out a copy of *Angel Times* and showed me the article about her interview called "Sacred Geometry, Baseball & Angels." Fascinating, and now I believed.

Shona the Olympics Drummer and Dancer

The day I met Shona I saw some rare Olympic collectible pins on the wall, pins given only to a select few. Shona casually mentioned that she and her roommate, Sherry Wheat, had danced and drummed in the opening ceremony at the 1996 Centennial Summer Olympic Games in Atlanta. (She also sang in the opening ceremony of the Paralympic Games.)

She did not know that I was there at the games but could not get those sold-out tickets. Nor did she know that my University of Georgia classmate, Billy Payne, was head of the Olympic Committee, the same man Shona met to pitch her ideas. With Shona, over and over it seemed I was one person away from knowing famous people. I gradually came to realize the power of her charm that took my breath away.

As long as I knew Shona, she displayed her Olympic costume on a mannequin in her home and ours. It was gold and black and had a full face mask so that all the performers could represent all of humankind, regardless of age, sex, or color. She also kept her mallets for the giant drums she beat high off the ground. Shona was very proud of that accomplishment.

She told me that the choreographer, Kenny Ortega, gathered them together just after the bombing that day in Atlanta and just before performing. In an atmosphere of great uncertainty, he said that any of them could just walk away to their families and he would understand. All chose to stay. As a combat veteran, I understood that communal commitment to a higher purpose.

After the Olympics, a group of Shona and others was hired to perform at private venues, a testament to their collective talent. Her friend, Sherry Wheat, writes more about their experience.

I had been drumming in a percussion choir when I met Shona and we decided to rent a house together on Spalding Drive in Dunwoody, Georgia. I had been performing in a percussion tribe led by Chuck Cogliandro, a noted artist and leader of the Kumandi Drum Circle that did African drumming for creativity, deep connection, and healing. The tribe had already performed for three Presidents. Chuck selected the 100 volunteers for the Olympic opening ceremony without regard for age, sex, or color. Shona said she was interested and got it without an audition because I vouched for her. Kenny Ortega organized and trained us and choreographed the music by Mickey Hart (former Grateful Dead drummer). At the time, her children, Serena and Adin, were also living with us and at times some of the volunteer drummers stayed at our house.

We started practicing in April or May. I remember the distinctive way Kenny led us. He was a constant and consistent proponent of positive feedback encouraging us amateurs to grow past our mistakes as we learned the music and moves.

There were separate dancers on the field. We drummed and danced our way to each drumming tower, then ascended, and drummed up there.

After our performance, I helped Shona with her kiosk, selling T-shirts of her paintings.

Following the summer games, Shona and I performed in the Atlanta 1996 Paralympics in the same stadium (later repurposed for baseball, I think). It was televised for the first time and had celebrity support from people like Christopher

Reeve, who hosted the games. We wore yellow tunics, but the greatest contrast was the lack of security and the lack of positive feedback from the directors in our drumming practices.

From time to time, a few of us were asked to drum for private occasions. That was a confirmation of our group talent.

But I am sure Shona would agree with me that the opening ceremony was a fabulous and amazing night! One of my greatest thrills was walking out onto the field before 86,000 roaring people.

The Olympics were an amazing two weeks of love energy unlike anything I have ever experienced. That love permeated and unified the whole of Atlanta, much like the aftermath of 9/11 in New York City. And it certainly confirmed Shona's love and hope for mankind that was already there.

Shona the Ski Instructor

Shona and Richard had skied in the Alps on their honeymoon and I assumed she was already an accomplished skier as she told me she had been a ski instructor before we met.

In 2014, during my grandson River's spring break, we took him to the Cataloochee Ski Resort in Maggie Valley, North Carolina. There Shona taught him the rudiments of snowboarding. (Later, we bought him his own snowboard.)

She also took the lift to the top and skied down. Out of my sight, she crashed, but picked herself up in typical Shona fashion and finished the run smiling.

Years earlier, I had concluded that Shona could do whatever she set her mind to do. Once again, this wonder woman that I loved proved that to be so and created an indelible memory with a grandchild of mine.

Shona the Hostage

Shona only told me this story one time, but I'll try to relate what she told me as accurately as I can.

Shona was flying with her boyfriend, Grahame, either to or from India, after she had divorced Richard. On the flight were many Indian families and children. They made an intermediate stop. I deduced it was probably in Tajikistan. Once they landed, they were escorted under armed guard to an unused terminal building. The guards were very young, nervous, inexperienced, and armed (likely with AK-47s). All the passengers were herded into a single large room. They could see through a metal grate into the adjoining room, probably a food service area, because Shona could see cases of Coca-Cola stacked in the back.

They were without food or water and none of the guards could speak the languages of the passengers. On the third day, Shona could sense that the babies were constantly crying because they were hungry. The mothers were getting upset and their husbands were getting very upset, chattering away in their native tongue. Shona could not understand them, but she understood their increasingly volatile emotions were about to erupt and possibly trigger a massacre by the nervous guards.

Shona, being Shona, took the matter in her own hands. She confronted the guards, screaming and gesturing with her hands to communicate they needed something to drink. She pointed to the Cokes and they refused. Undeterred, she kept up her protest. Then she noticed that a doorway to the drinks was unlocked.

So Shona, shaking inside, confidently walked in and simply took a case. The guards were completely flabbergasted. Apparently, they had never experienced such a powerful, assertive woman and did not know what to do about it. So they stood by and did nothing.

Shona set up a chain of men and they quickly brought the warm soft drinks for all the passengers, averting a potential catastrophe.

They all eventually boarded the same aircraft again and completed their flight. Later, Shona somehow learned that the mujahedeen had commandeered the airplane to run guns to Afghanistan.

Again I concluded that this woman I loved could not have made this up and had no reason for doing so. She was already amazing enough.

Shona the Educator

In addition to her far-flung global adventures, Shona somehow found time to continue to educate herself and to reach out and share her knowledge with others. Remember that Shona was given minimal education while she was growing up and never went to college. She admitted that she didn't learn to read well until she was 25 years old.

In 1978, while living in Greenwich, Connecticut, Shona began teaching Mechanical Engineering and Aerodynamics with grades 7-9 at The Mead School. She was also responsible, with a small group of people, for fundraising that resulted in a $1,000,000 donation to the school. Shona participated in curriculum design and in forming a Parent Center Network to provide backup skills for the teachers using qualified parental help.

During this time, Shona began studying Whole Brain Learning with Elaine De Beauport, the founder of The Mead School, incorporating her knowledge into the school curriculum and into her seminars. She was also exploring all the healing techniques that she later used in her counseling work.

In 1980, Shona designed and presented seminars on various aspects of self-development and self-healing with a colleague, Melissa Schnirring, in Westport, Connecticut. The courses covered subjects such as:

The Empowerment of Women
How to Get to the Top and Still Be Feminine
Intuitive Thinking in Leadership
Left/Right Brain Training
Prospering Women: A Workshop on Abundance

Relationship Awareness Training:
   A New Way to Relate to People at Home and at Work
Heal Thyself: Taking Responsibility for Your Health and
   Well-being.

In 1984 the Bellew family returned to England where Shona formed a company called Mead Research into Education Ltd. with Jonathan Wolf-Philips. Together they researched British educational systems and later began a new form of schooling in partnership with Philip Toogood, a well-known teacher in the field of forward-looking education. The Dame Catherine School was formed to be a replaceable answer to the growing problem of oversized classes and a lack of community integration with the British educational system. It was reviewed in the London Times Educational Supplement and the Manchester Guardian Educational Supplement as a sensible way of providing a better class of education, particularly in the rural districts of the U.K.

A few years later, Shona was invited to join the group, Technologies for Change, a forward-looking management training group in London. With a wide variety of clients such as The Rover Car Company, The London Stock Exchange, Ogilvy and Mather Advertising, and P.A. Consultants, Shona was able to experience many different aspects of the business world. She gained many insights and developed a number of valuable skills. She designed and presented specific training courses in Whole Brain Learning such as:

Leadership Skills for the 21st Century
Sales Training
Marketing Strategies
Interdepartmental Relationships
Fear in the Workplace
The Hidden Saboteur

In 1991, after her divorce, Shona came back to the U.S. as a single parent to work for The National Academy of Integrative

104

Learning in Rochester, New York. With Peter Kline and his group, she presented seminars on Integrative Learning for Eastman Kodak. Then, in 1994, Shona created a company with four other consultants called Future Connection. This organization was set up to present leadership seminars and workshops on 'Creating Your Own Tools to be a Genius Thinker!'

Shona | 1995
© Tricia McCannon

Shona also was a lecturer, along with Deepak Chopra, at the 5th Annual Kaua'i Wellness Expo in January of 2009. Her presentation, titled "Immortality and Leadership: Creative Empowerment Through the Divine" presented her theory of what she called 'Big Toe Living' to create a life of fulfillment.

Shona the Doll Designer

Shona never stopped thinking of ways to make the world a better place, especially for young people. She truly believed that the early dreams and visions of children retained their magic even into old age.

> *I have discovered that the things that make me the most happy now are the dreams unfolding that I had as a child and grew to believe would never be realized because they were smothered by stronger adults around me. They made me believe that my childhood fantasies were silly and unreal.*

In 1997, she and a dear friend began thinking about a special doll that would help people access and heal their inner child, but her friend became too busy and Shona went ahead by herself.

> *"Be ye as little children to enter the kingdom of heaven." This quote from the Bible has finally made sense to me. The doll is a gateway back to who you really are, where your heart really resides, and what you came here to be and do. It is simple and effective. My design is a spatial mathematical language that the left brain, our judge, cannot cross off.*

Shona and I further developed the idea and completed a provisional application for a patent.

We called it 'The Magical Me Doll System' and described it as an integrated therapeutic system for self-help based on an interactive doll that represents and resembles the owner when the owner was younger. The purpose of the MMDS is for the owner to remind or remember who you really were before you got changed into someone else.

I envisioned the dolls as all cloth, custom hand-made, with the imprinted photo of the client on the face. They would be about nine inches tall and very portable. Shona would dress them in clothes patterned with her geometric art. The doll would entitle the owner to individual therapy via a website that would connect them to cooperating therapists in their local area as well as related books, workshops, and audio tapes.

We eventually tabled the project because of the overwhelming business aspects. Neither one of us had any business experience and we would have had to hire a patent attorney. I think it is still a valid idea and if Shona were alive, I have no doubt that we would have manifested it.

Shona the Bricklayer & Stone Circle Architect

About a year after her daughter Serena was born, Shona and Richard began building a homestead on Salterns Lane in Hampshire, England. During the bricklayers' strike, Shona became certified as a bricklayer and proceeded, on her own, to build their boiler house.

In 2015, after Shona had been living at the foot of a mountain outside Crozet, Virginia, she decided to have her own stone circle in the front yard, similar to Stonehenge. She got permission from her landlord, another Brit she had charmed.

On her many walks in the woods, she gradually found all the stones she needed. Each one was about the size of a barrel. The landlord's handyman, a big, gentle, burly man, brought a small Caterpillar loader and together they crashed out many paths in the woods and brought back the stones. I have to imagine the process since I only saw the finished result.

After construction, Shona invited like-minded friends to celebrate the solstice and equinox and dance with her in the circle. It did not surprise me later on when Serena spread Shona's ashes at historic Castlerigg Stone Circle in northwest England, a place we had visited together a year after we first met.

Castlerigg Stone Circle
© Serena Bellew Welshans

Shona's Stone Circle | 2015

Anonymous Dancer at Shona's Stone Circle

Shona the Actress

It's almost hard to believe, but in addition to her regular appearances on radio, Shona somehow had the time to devote to Shakespearean theater, film, television, and industrial commercials.

She appeared in a number of plays in both the U.S. and U.K., playing Gwenivere in "Camelot" for the Stroud Actors Guild as well as a non-speaking bit part in the MGM production of "Fled."

As a member of The Delphi Players, she wrote and performed plays with a spiritual message. She was also an extra on the American prime time soap opera "Savannah" on the WB network.

While living in Greenwich, Connecticut, Shona also directed and acted with children of all ages at The Mead School.

Shona as a Goddess & Gangster | October 2001

Shona the Writer

In mid-life, Shona decided to devote herself to writing. Although she had already written many proposals and articles for New Age magazines and journals, she felt an intense desire to tell her life story.

As she said in her journal:

> *I have an incredible bank of wisdom and knowledge on so many subjects but all in my head, unknown and intangible in*

the outside world. How I long for a tangible document that I could hold in my hands and say this is me, Shona, look and enjoy. Not only my wisdom but my story and my life are important to put down in a document.

She was very specific about what she wanted to accomplish. On January 19, 1999, at 1:27 p.m. her diary entry read:

I want to write about me mostly. I want to write about my life story, the idea of three strands of writing, fact or reality, fantasy and magic. Then I want to weave them together so that you can't tell one from the other. I want to write about my life for a screenplay or TV series, I want to write it as a soap opera, or drama like that. I want to write about Genesis, the story of the Garden of Eden mythology and the experiment of life. I want to write about health and healing of the body and how to do it. I want to write about losing weight, self-help books, a whole series on health and healing, finding the little kid, power, creativity. I want to write about people living the lives they want, about childhood techniques to leave them alone. I want to write training manuals for companies and sports teams, and do the training.

I want to write about leadership and what the new leader means. I want to write about future science ideas, unified field theories, and my notions of time and space, etc. I want to publish a scientific book on my ideas. I want to write about how to have a genius mind understanding. I want to write about men, what is the modern day warrior? I want to write about women, what the new unfolding Goddess looks like. I want to write about my art and explain the new spatial mathematics of the future.

I want to invent new scientific projects and then write about them. I want to write about a new community development scheme, new factories, and how to run them. I want to write children's books for wisdom and insight, coupled with the dolls. I want to write little kid workbooks and other workbooks. I want to write a TV show about people and have insights and answers that grow awareness. I want to write board games for self-development that are as good as Trivial Pursuit. I want to write publishable poetry books on love, danger, joy, etc. I want to write beautiful coffee table books of my art and writings. I want to write articles in famous magazines. I want to write articles for scientific journals. I want to write about the future of this planet and how to solve various problems.

I want to write a comedy like <u>Monty Python</u> and have it be a TV series. I want to write a show like <u>South Park</u>. I want to write a series of brilliant ads for TV, setting a new intelligent type of advertising that does no harm but catches on. I want to write about the mythology of life, the characters we are and how they interact. I want to write a <u>Star Wars</u>-type series of books about my knowledge of space beings and their higher ways. I want to write about love and how to tell it, find it, and keep it.

I want to write a handbook for looking after babies and children. I want to write newsletters and magazines to promote my company. I want to write cards, calendars, and posters for people to feel good. I want to write out-of-the-box funny books for adults and children. I want to write about angels and phenomena, ET and fairies, adventures that little ones recognize and so do adults, with beautiful art, too. I want to write <u>Celestine Prophecy</u>-type books that are simple, spiritual, and easy to read. I want to write angel stories to show how to see them. I want to write stories like <u>Phenomenon</u> to stretch people's minds. I want to always write for the sheer fun of it and I want to get paid a lot for what I write for the people, as I will write about myself and all that I AM.

As with every aspect of her journey, Shona had perfect trust that the universe would provide.

I panic sometimes as there is so much to write and I wonder how to compartmentalize it all. Which book first, etc., then I realize that all I have to do is write. The future will show me how to market the material and somehow they will fall into place of their own accord.

In 2003, Shona went to Belize for a month to write. She may have realized that it would take the rest of her lifetime to complete all the things she wanted to do, but I wonder if she suspected then that it would become my own mission to share her life story with the world?

Jay & Shona | 1998
Unknown Photographer

Chapter Nine

Our Marriage

**In the season of now
we have found what all lovers seek,
the truth of two:
in loving is being;
in living is seeing;
and from connection
comes all creation.**

Living with Shona was so easy. I loved her passionately, erotically, physically. And that gradually grew into something even better. "This, or something better," she always told me.

Shona wrote this pledge to me on December 19, 1999.

You cannot possess me for I belong to myself.
But while we both wish it, I give you that which is mine to give.
You cannot command me for I am a free person.
But I shall serve you in those ways of love you require:
the honeycomb will taste sweeter anyway from my hand.
I pledge to you that yours will be the eyes into which I smile each morning.
I pledge to you the first kiss of each day.
I pledge to you to be a shield to your back and you to mine.

I pledge to honor and respect you for who you are.
I pledge to see your innocence in all moments
because I accept my own always.
I pledge to create a space of peace and tranquility
and balance in our lives together.
I pledge to always tell the truth to myself and you.
You, Jay, and none other shall be my partner in life's journey
as long as our hearts sing together.

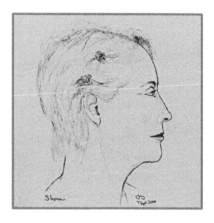

**Shona
on Our Wedding Day**

She once asked, "Jay, who would you choose if given free choice: me, or me without any of my flaws?" A classic Southern gentleman, I said I would remain loyal to the you I know. She replied, "Are you deceiving yourself?"

She forced me to ponder the same question in reverse. Of course, I would want her to choose the unflawed Jay. Thus I had to choose the unflawed Shona.

"See, now you understand why the universe is always in flow seeking balance. This or something better." I had never encountered a woman, anyone, with such deep wisdom. She was already a blessing to me in the guise of a drop-dead gorgeous woman. (She once replied back that I was a drop-dead handsome man. Ha!)

Everything just flowed. And time flew, too. Life was a banquet of ourselves. Here is a portrait of a day, what happened when we were simply together.

> *Evening has come, and I sit on the back porch feeling gratitude. She joins me soon and we talk of the mundane and the profane and of the love we keep growing together. But mostly, we just enjoy the company of each another. She is still so interesting to talk to. Her mind is so creative, so outrageously funny, so intelligent, and so open. Her body still stiffens me and I love the mature way she looks in and out of clothes.*
>
> *The greatest appeal to me remains her spirit and connection with the universe. I learn so much from just knowing and loving her. Time and again I find that she is simply a mirror to my own wisdom I have yet to see. Conversation with her is the closest I've come to enlightenment. We withhold nothing and hold each other close discussing the stars.*
>
> *Later we retire to bed, each in our own private thoughts of the blessings of the day. Before sleep embraces us, we soothe each other's bodies with tantric touches. We giggle and moan and play for a while, going nowhere in particular. We manifest again in our minds the oldest truth, that all there is, is love. Love is the light and we are the light as well. We end up with me inside my goddess, and I slowly float into enchantment again knowing another day awaits.*

We married on March 22, 2000 in the Hamilton County Courthouse in Chattanooga, Tennessee. We wrote and spoke our own vows:

Jay & Shona | Marriage Vows

Spoken One to The Other | Shona & Jay

You are the love I choose and I choose to share
  my future with you.

With all my passion, I love and honor you as I love and honor me.
I honor the sacredness of me and the sacredness of you.
I play and celebrate my life which I choose to share with you
I live in the now, not in the past, not in the future,
  and I do it with you.
I nurture our togetherness and value our separateness.
I am there for the best of you, the worst of you,
  and all of you in between.
I make love to you and no other.
I live my truth, for that is what makes my heart sing and expands
  my joy of you.
I am your spiritual soul mate for as long as my heart
  sings with yours.
We are our own best friends. We share the same deepest values.
We trust who we are and each other. We share all dreams and fears
  in truth and trust, without withholding or waiting. We do not
  judge each other, even as we learn to stop judging ourselves.
We help each other get what we want. We allow miracles and
  wonder to connect us to the universe of our own creation.

I adore you.

Spoken by the Minister

[Extract from *The Prophet* – On Marriage – by Kahlil Gibran]

You were born together, and together you shall be
  forevermore…
But let there be spaces in your togetherness, and let the
  winds of the heavens dance between you…
Sing and dance together and be joyous, but let each one
  of you be alone, even as the strings of a lute are alone
  though they quiver with the same music…
Give your hearts, but not into each other's keeping…
And stand together yet not too near together:
For the pillars of the temple stand apart, and the oak tree
  and the cypress grow not in each other's shadow.

Spoken by Jay to Shona
[To My Real You by Jay Harden, 16 Feb 99]

I want to marry the real you,
Whoever that is.
Whatever in you that is real
Is what I want to love.
More than the false faces,
Others spaces,
The pretend graces
You were taught to show,
Times ago.

Tell me of your truth,
And when you were young
Making every mistake.

See me listen well,
Hearing nothing wrong,
And let me cause you smiles
In every moment's pause.

Share your hours
And your fears,
And watch me still adore you.

Disclose your soul to mine,
And we will gain
Protection from the cold.

And take from me
All of me,
The salt
As well as the steam.
Surrender with me
Every delight,
In every kiss exchanged.

Linger with me always
In the fully present now,

And know that tomorrow
Is only
Now extended.

World of our owning,
Watch us demonstrate
That creation lives
In us and all
We dare breathe upon.

Shona and I agreed from the beginning to full disclosure and honesty. We always kept our promises with each other. That was liberating far beyond what we could have imagined and is perhaps our proudest achievement. From that flowed the deepest friendship, respect, and love we have ever known. Her trust in me, even when we divorced, never wavered.

As time went by, Shona and I continued to have many adventures, both by ourselves and together. While Shona went alone to Belize to write in the summer of 2003, I went to India. When I returned, she wrote this in her journal.

I don't think he hears me when I say I still love him very much, but I can see the journey that both of us must take, so I cannot even have expectations about the future which makes it harder. There has to be a break now so that I can complete my healing and so can he. The future is in the hands of the I AM Presence.

Wow. I see the love we have for each other and the catalyst that it has been for healing. I see now how I could not have done it any other way. I think once we are over the pain of separating we will see and be able to appreciate our love and its power to heal.

Thank you Jay for your love that has held the space for me to grow and heal the old wounds. I really appreciate what you have done for me, and I do see why we signed the contract to do this together for we do have a very, very deep love that has gone through a lot of lifetimes. It is a great gift.

My understanding is that Shona faced a choice in our marriage. She could either continue working with me daily on my trauma issues, sacrificing her own needs, or she could focus on her trauma issues at a distance from my pain. I saw the wisdom in her decision to live independently so she could work intensely on her deeper wounding. It was hard for her to ask for what she really needed, afraid I would stop being her friend and the great love of her life. I sadly and bravely agreed to give up her presence and her touch.

This took the greatest trust in each other.

Jay & Shona
Our Wedding Day | March 22, 2000
Unknown Photographer

Chapter Ten

Our Divorce

I've learned from this a law, my love,
across the universe:
we see outside what is within—
our best from loving first.

How is it possible for two people to love each other, divorce, and be even more in love with each other? Conventional wisdom says there is no such thing as an amicable divorce. But, if there was, wouldn't it be a hope to many?

In April of 2006, a few months before our divorce, I wrote her this letter:

My dear Shona,

I have just talked to you on your birthday. If there were only some words I could say, some way to let you know the truth of my soul, then you would feel better, and me, too. I hear in your voice and words the deep wounding that has destroyed the last beautiful thing we had together. So many significant events/decisions have happened to me in the last few days. They do not compare to the loss of your friendship that I finally destroyed unwittingly. I would beg for your forgiveness and grace if I knew what to beg for. I pray with all my heart that your life is full of deserved happiness and peace and that, in time, you find some perfection in me—enough to make you smile once more—the same perfection I am seeking, too. I already see yours; I always did, it was so easy. I'm not sure if I am destined to ever see you again, but I will always see you in my mind's eye, ever the Giggles in a tree house. You were the blessing of my life and I always wanted to be the same for you. There is only one way to end this letter and that is with . . .

Love, love, always love,
Jay

When we married, we promised to stay together "as long as our hearts sing together." In our marriage, I was not aware of my increasing emotional dependence upon Shona as my personal therapist for my many traumas at the expense of Shona working on her many more. She was sacrificing her healing for mine. When she told me this, it was unacceptable to us both. Shona moved to a rental house at the top of a mountain in northeast Georgia to work on herself, and eventually told me her divine inner wisdom said we must formally end our marriage.

I was crushed, of course, but did not want to be married to someone who did not want to be married to me. I volunteered to continue her financial support so she would never fear being homeless ever again.

Our divorce lawyer was incredulous, and our children were furious and could not understand. The fault was not in us, but in our crushing childhoods. We wanted to heal ourselves as an example to our children. We knew there are no mistakes in the universe and that our destinies were forever entwined.

We divorced on June 20, 2006 in Clarke County, Athens, Georgia. As when we married, we wrote and held a private divorce ceremony, crying and smiling the whole time. After the divorce, we made each other executors of our wills, which dismayed our children.

We stayed married in spirit, and over the years I proposed marriage again to Shona many times, each gentle declination a crush to my heart that my loneliness and longing for her presence had to accept. I kept relearning the lesson of living in the present moment only.

I do not pretend to have some ancient wisdom to explain all this to myself or the outer world. I just know that Shona and I were blessed with a profound and beautiful love that endures beyond formal marriage and this existence.

Jay & Shona | June 2006
Unknown Photographer

Chapter Eleven

Travels with Shona

They traveled the byways (she drove very fast)
and slayed all their secrets and conquered the past.
She practiced her art; he wrote his heart out;
a curious couple to strangers, no doubt.

Chuck Visits Shona

I met Chuck Eisenberg in early 2007 in a Vietnam veteran therapy group after I moved to O'Fallon, Missouri. Soon after, Shona came to visit me and my daughter's family next door and wanted to meet my new friends. Shona loved to entertain, so she hosted a dinner party for Mike and Debbie and Chuck and Brenda in my tiny kitchen. They still talk of that dinner party to this day, remembering my unforgettable Shona and the fabulous meal she prepared.

Chuck liked to drive, and he liked road trips. One we took with Shona while she was living in Virginia after being diagnosed with rectal cancer made such an impression on Chuck that he wrote this:

> *I always enjoyed getting together with Shona and Jay. She truly was a one-of-a-kind person to me. I'd never met a Brit before, and noble born to boot. She always appeared a little larger*

than life and in complete control of her surroundings. No surprise for a lady raised to run the manor.

I have many pleasant memories of the times the three of us spent together, but one in particular stands out. Jay and I had driven to Charlottesville and Shona suggested she give us a tour of the town, followed by dinner. So we piled into Jay's RAV4, he at the wheel, Shona at shotgun, and me in the back seat.

During the ride I had a smoke, then reached for my roll of breath mints. I asked if either of them would care for one. Shona perked up and said, "What's a breath mint?" At first I thought she was kidding, but she insisted she'd never had one. Jay declined but Shona put out her hand, then popped it into her mouth.

All of a sudden, Shona bolted upright and 'screamed' something unintelligible. Jay asked if she was alright and she hollered, "This is like a hot coal!" She began gagging and choking like it was caught in her throat. But it couldn't have been because she was still shrieking words of displeasure and begging what to do with the worst thing she'd ever tasted. More uncontrollable writhing and, after what seemed like an eternity, the offensive lozenge was finally out of her mouth and in her hand. NOW WHAT TO DO? Quick on his feet, Jay lowered the passenger window and the ordeal was finally over.

After a few 'bloody'-filled sentences, Shona fully recovered. Meanwhile, Jay and I exploded in laughter, the heavy kind that lasts for awhile. Jay did attempt to explain the breath mint concept, but Shona was not interested.

Reliving that experience with Shona and Jay after that day always brought smiles and giggles to our faces. It still does for Jay and me.

Chuck supported me with his presence at Shona's celebration of her life. Now, *he* is my best friend and we continue to take road trips whenever we can.

Shona in Italy

In August of 2011, Shona and I took our first international adventure together to Italy. We went to Florence first and walked the same streets as Michelangelo. We saw his statue of David and some of his unfinished works. My jaw dropped seeing it and I remembered how he said of his process, that he merely removed the unwanted stone to uncover what was already there. I fell in love with the city and its palazzos, wanting to live there someday.

As a photographer, I people-watched from a sidewalk café. As in the States, I averted my eyes when females walking by caught me staring. I soon learned that this offended Italian women. They like to be noticed and exchanged smiles with me as I appreciated their elegant clothes and confident walking. What a different experience from America!

We visited the Hotel Savoia where Shona's father met his brother during WWII and saw each other for the last time, six days before her father was killed behind the lines under suspicious circumstances. Shona chose not to travel the short distance to see her father's grave in the Forli War Cemetery.

We took a side trip from Florence to Sienna and a Mediterranean beach full of bikinis and Speedos. Two days later we took the train to Rome. Shona was my driver, tour guide, and translator. We darted around in a tiny Fiat Cinquecento. In Vatican City, I glimpsed the incredible Pietà behind bulletproof glass.

As we toured St. Peter's Square, Shona told me of her short time in 1964 on holiday in Rome with her husband Richard. She met Colonel Corsani, the head of Vatican security, who took her on a personal tour of the Vatican that included secret doors and priceless Renaissance art on the floor leaning casually against the walls, all visually overwhelming to her. We were unable to contact Corsani, now a retired General.

Of course, we saw the Forum, the Colosseum, the Circus Maximus, and walked the Via Appia. I was very disappointed that the Sistine Chapel was closed and we could not see the restored frescos. The breathtaking Pantheon was my favorite. Its grandeur spoke to me. It was so wonderful to share travels with the most beautiful and loving woman in my life.

Shona in Rome

Shona in England

Life with Shona was never dull. When Shona and I first traveled to England, she arranged for me to meet Uncle Henry, her favorite relative. He invited us for lunch at the Carlton Club.

I told Shona I was going to wear my best suit with a white shirt to show off the RAF tie I bought for the occasion. "God, no, a white shirt is considered common here." So I wore a light blue shirt.

We took a taxi and walked in under a sign consisting of three ostrich feathers, showing that the patron of this gentleman's club was Prince Charles. There was no outside marker identifying the club on Saint James. We were shown up a magnificent staircase, much like the one in *Gone with the Wind*. On the landing was a larger-than-life portrait of the Queen in a shimmering blue gown.

We were escorted to a corner table beneath a huge portrait of Sir William Pitt painted by Sir Joshua Reynolds. Over in another corner was a former Prime Minister smoking a cigar and reading the Times in his leather chair. I had to keep my jaw from dropping. I kept looking around for cameras. It seemed like I was walking on the set of a James Bond movie. The place was dripping in history.

Lieutenant-General Sir Henry Leask was waiting for us in a pin-striped suit, purple shirt, and pointy Italian shoes, looking to me like a dapper *mafioso*. We instantly hit it off. Uncle Henry was on Montgomery's staff in North Africa and then participated in the landing at Anzio, winning the Distinguished Service Order. He also became the head of all British Army training, the Commanding General of Scotland, Governor of Edinburgh Castle, and, after retirement, personal financial advisor to Queen Elizabeth. He also founded the Clan Leask Society.

There were at least three waiters attending to us and absolutely fawning over Uncle Henry. There was no menu or price list, so they announced the fare for the day, including the grouse flown in from Scotland.

Lieutenant-General Sir Henry Leask
Unknown Artist

Shona chose the fish and Uncle Henry chose the grouse. I was always taught you can't go wrong if you choose to follow the host. Shona knew what I was thinking and kicked my shin under the table. But I had never tried grouse so I said, "I believe I will take the grouse also." She kicked me again and my leg began to smart.

Our conversation was delightful, and Shona was charming in her familiar element. Then came my grouse. It was bloody and gamey, decidedly an acquired taste. Shona gave me that look but didn't kick me again. As I did as a child, I ate the best edges and rearranged my plate to look like I had overeaten and was finished.

The impertinent head waiter leaned forward and sniffed, "Sir, was the grouse not to your liking?" I paused for the right words, then said, "It was . . . adequate." I meant no disrespect. Shona really kicked me this time. Now my leg was throbbing, but I didn't wince. The waiter blanched and took my words as a personal insult. Of course, Uncle Henry pretended not to hear this exchange. Our table conversation continued, every word overhead by the waiters standing over our shoulders the entire meal.

I later learned about grouse. The dead grouse shot on the moors of Scotland is hung by the head until the body falls off. Then it is ripe enough to eat for aristocrats. Fish and chips are commoner fare.

Then came the after dinner drinks. Uncle Henry chose the port and curious me chose to try it, too. Another kick and I wondered if my leg was bleeding.

The port came in a huge goblet. It reminded me of Mark Twain's explanation of the Missouri River: "It's too thick to drink and too thin to plow." I could manage only a few slow and polite sips.

The three of us departed to the street. Uncle Henry drew Shona aside and whispered, "That Jay, he's all right . . . for an American." His driver opened the door and we hailed a taxi.

As you might imagine, Shona had some words for me. "You probably cost the head waiter his job, or the chef, or both." I was stunned and will never know the consequences of my honesty. To me, Uncle Henry was a true gentleman, fellow combat warrior, and my friend, and I was honored that Shona chose to introduce me to him and to view her aristocratic origins up close.

Shona & My Grandchildren

Before I met Shona and after the birth of my first grandchild, I resolved to give each of my grandchildren a grand adventure with me at my expense, something to remember me by after I am gone. When I told Shona about my dreamed adventures, she was in complete agreement with my idea.

When he was 10, I gave my eldest grandson, River, a rafting trip through the Grand Canyon. My daughter, Camilla, convinced my son, Ben, to go with us. That made it all the more fun and reassured my daughter that her son would be safe.

We three guys spent the first day at a dude ranch on the rim and shot skeet. The next day we took a helicopter ride to the floor of the canyon where our rubber rafts waited. The copter took off and made a nosedive straight into the canyon, the safest and quickest way down. It was River's first chopper ride and he turned white as a sheet, while I was elated.

The next morning, we got into our 30-person rafts. The three of us sat in the back near the helmsman, but soon I ventured to the front end of the raft and Ben followed. It was glorious to bend up and down over the rapids, yell, and get splashed by the Colorado River. Soon enough, as I hoped, River joined us. I think it was a brave turn in his ten-year-old life.

The Grand Canyon is a living thing and no photography can do justice to its majesty. I watched a side calve into the river, changing before my eyes. I was a privileged witness to the evolving universe that was changing me, too, as I watched my grandson grow past his fears.

That night we camped on the riverbank under the stars as our guides cooked a feast of manly steaks and all the trimmings. I was on my back asleep on my cot when the full moon broke over the lip of the canyon. I felt the light on my eyelids and thought it must be the sun telling me to get up. I opened my eyes and saw this beautiful golden orb, a vista equal in its own way to the stars at 40,000 feet over the Pacific on a Vietnam combat mission.

We did two more days of this until we arrived at Lake Mead, then flew home. Ben decided he would take his son on this trip when he got old enough.

Shona adored River and all my children and grandchildren. River was impressed with Shona, too. During one visit in 2016, Shona and I watched as River and his friends built a potato gun out of PVC pipe, with hair spray as the propellant and piezoelectric ignition.

River, Ben, & Shona

Shona and I were itching to try. At last, River offered me a shot. I took aim at a wood pile about 100 feet away. I missed, but hit the top of Camilla's chicken coop with five chickens inside. The official BDA was zero chickens and eggs damaged. Camilla was inside at the time; we didn't tell her until a few days later.

Shona fired it, too. She earned her shot as the former adult advisor to the Rocket Club of The Mead School in Greenwich, Connecticut. We continued until Camilla's refrigerator gave up its last spud.

River later included this adventure with Shona in his college scholarship application, writing "There is probably a potato patch growing back in our woods somewhere."

When River's sister, Maia, was 12 I asked her where she wanted to go on her adventure. She said she wanted to see the Eiffel Tower, so Shona and I took her.

Shona, having lived in Paris, was the perfect companion for Maia, who was frightened and overwhelmed by this foreign country and being so far away from her mother. We thought we might have to turn around and return home, but Maia considered Shona like a second mother and overcame her fear. In those nine days I watched her grow a strength of spirit before my eyes, mentored by Shona. She fell in love with Paris, particularly the baguettes and hot chocolate in the sidewalk cafés. She was so pleased (Shona would say 'chuffed') to pour the milk and chocolate to suit her taste.

Shona took her to buy shoes and a beret as I patiently endured their giggling shopping, then we went one of the Paris open air markets to buy fresh food and bread.

We went to the Louvre and Maia had to confront the marble nudity of *Venus de Milo*. I got to see my favorites, *The Winged Victory of Samothrace* and *Mona Lisa* (much smaller than I expected). We also found a statue of King Edward III, a common ancestor of Shona's children and my son's wife.

Maia in Paris

Maia was served a nearly raw hamburger in the 600-year-old house of Nicolas Flamel, a character in the Harry Potter series. She stood in her power and sent it back to the kitchen.

While we were waiting outside to tour the Paris Opera, I encountered a sophisticated con artist as Maia watched. The attractive, sincere-acting woman surreptitiously dropped a gold wedding ring at my feet, then pointed to it, and asked if it was mine, hoping my greed would prevail and I would say yes. Then, of course, she would wait patiently for her reward. But I sensed what was going on and said no. She walked away and I picked up a plastic ring. She disappeared into the crowd, no doubt with a pocket full of others. It was a great lesson for Maia, one she has never forgotten.

Then we went to Versailles and I was overwhelmed by the vast gardens.

We managed to find where Shona once lived on Avenue Klebér in the 16th Arrondissement and watched the French Foreign Legion march down the Champs-Élysées on their Veteran's Day.

At Notre Dame, Maia lit a candle for her grandmother Carolyn, then we crossed the Seine and visited the favorite bookstore of Hemingway's, *Shakespeare and Company*, where I had to buy a book of his with the bookstore stamp. We got to see Rodin's home and *The Thinker* in his garden. Maia was thrilled to watch *The Hunger Games* movie (in English with French subtitles) before it was released in America. I enjoyed the massive water lilies paintings of Monet and was chastised by the staff for taking a photograph.

When we got to the Eiffel Tower, Maia was intimidated by its size and decided not to go up. I told her I wasn't traveling 4,000 miles across the ocean to just stand at the foot of the Eiffel Tower. I was going up. Again, bravery overcame fear and we three took the elevator. Shona and I drank champagne and kissed at the top as we surveyed all of Paris.

On our last night, Maia and I, at her insistence, walked the streets past the embassies—without Shona. Her new self-confidence was amazing. I watched my granddaughter grow from a little girl into her own self before my eyes. I knew it when she said it was better than a year of school. But my greatest reward was when Maia told me, "GJ, when I grow up, I'm going to take *you* to Paris!" The secret success of this trip was due, of course, to that magical woman, my Shona, infecting all of us with unfettered joy.

A few years passed, and it was my granddaughter Journey's turn. When she was 11, I asked her where she wanted to go on an adventure with Shona and me. She had heard from Shona's daughter, Serena, that The Making of Harry Potter studio tour outside London was worth the trip. So we went to what was once the world's largest aircraft factory during World War II. Interestingly, my daughter, Camilla, wanted to go, too. She had never ventured outside the continental U.S. This time it was a foursome.

Shona found time to arrange a night bus tour of London, a boat cruise on the Thames, and high tea in Bath.

I can't say who had the most fun, Journey or Shona. They were both in their little kid mode the whole time, to my great delight. Camilla grew, too, and I think her courage led her to later pursue a graduate degree in social work.

Journey, Shona & Maia

I spent the six days surrounded by three beautiful women in my life acting like their hero.

Shona in Ireland

At last, it was our time to take our own adventure, just Shona and me, the last trip of two lovers.

Shona talked to me often of her love of Ireland, the lush greenness, and the fairies she could see there and the kind people who absolutely adore Americans. She wanted to show me. So in July of 2014 we flew over the pond. She drove us around, of course, but on the wrong side of the road. I merely grinned and held on.

We landed in Dublin and went to Adare Manor Castle in County Limerick. It was purchased by a former Marine A-4 fighter pilot in Vietnam, who renovated it.

Shona had an added purpose in going to Ireland. Over the years, long after Shona had forgiven Roderic, he would call her needing money. She loaned him several thousand that he never repaid, and she wanted to ask him about it in person. We drove to Sneem in County Kerry following detailed directions. No one seemed to be there, so I rang and rang a big bell hanging outside. Finally a woman appeared from another house and informed us Roderic was not there. He had waited for us the previous day. Shona's inner wisdom told her the wrong day and that we were not supposed to meet Roderic. I wanted very much to look in his eyes and read his energy field, a skill I had learned from Shona.

On our trip around the coast I was struck by the immaculate and colorful villages lovingly tended by the locals. Ireland is nothing like the drab and dirty gray photos in the history books of my school days.

"Tidy Towns" is a fierce annual competition across the country. There are substantial prizes for the winning towns which are reinvested in the community. Adare was the overall winner in 1976. This competition creates immense local pride and unexpected, substantial tourist income that is now a key part of Ireland's economy. (I could see their idea transplanted successfully in America.)

Driving around Ireland, we often stopped by the side of the road. Shona could see fairies, just like she did as a child. Her face and voice bubbled. We also visited Irish cemeteries that told of the brutal, random murders by the Black and Tans in the Irish War of Independence. Other headstones told of the Potato Famine of the 1840s, a deliberate attempt at genocide by the British causing an estimated 1,000,000 starvation deaths. About 2,000,000 survivors emigrated to the United States and the net Irish population fell by almost 25 per cent.

We were treated as honored American tourists by the Irish. They absolutely loved Americans and displayed the Stars and Stripes everywhere (but I saw not a single Union Jack). We could not have been treated better.

I wanted to go to a real Irish pub and hear them sing songs like "Danny Boy." I was surprised to find the locals around a table littered with musical instruments singing American traditional and country music. I knew every song and sang along with them to their delight and the delight of Shona. That was a memorable evening with free drinks.

Back at the manor by the River Maigue we found a gilley to take me flying fishing for trout. I succeeded near a magnificent 350-year-old cedar on the riverbank.

Our trip took us to Dingle Bay. Shona had told me that she had walked on fire and swam with dolphins, and I added those to my bucket list. We managed to find a boat that would take us out to swim with Fungie (foon-gay) the famous dolphin, the oldest known bottlenose dolphin in the world, and a minor Irish industry.

Fungie was first sighted in 1983 and absolutely thrives on human contact even though his home is the wild sea. He swims alongside boats, squeaks, and does flips in the air. Fungie and Shona swam together at least 25 years earlier. He and Shona were still in tune with each other. Perhaps he remembered her. I, on the other hand, nearly froze to death in a leaky wet suit and those very cold waters.

Then we drove the Ring of Kerry and stopped at a sloping cliff. Because of my heart attack, I elected to stay at the top while adventurous Shona worked her way down to the seaside boulders. I looked away, then back, and did not see her waving. Her body was face down, not moving. She did not respond to my voice. It was a good ten minutes down, and I realized I did not know if Ireland had a 911 number to call. I didn't know how to bring her up by myself, but I had to get down quickly and not slip on the loose shale. I had to look down every step while watching her and calling out. I wanted to avoid two casualties. No one else was around to help.

By the time I got to her, Shona had regained consciousness. Her face was bleeding and bruised, along with her upper torso. We climbed back up together very slowly. Back in Adare I inquired about a doctor, but Shona absolutely refused to go. We went to our rooms and I insisted we sleep with our doors open so I could hear her breathing. I got almost no sleep, fearing I would wake up in the morning to find her dead.

The next day we found The Homeopathic Clinic in Sneem and Shona treated herself. She asked me to photograph her wounds so she could monitor her healing.

When we returned home through the airport in Dublin, I discovered two separate security systems, something I had never seen. The Irish one was so long and inefficient I thought we would miss our flight. To my surprise, we then had to clear the American security system, apparently because it was a U.S. airline. I concluded we do not trust their security.

Our last international adventure together is now another wonderful memory. I rekindle it every now and then through the immortality of my photographs of Shona.

Chapter Twelve

Shona's Death

Would that the world knows you,
such is their need,
though incomparable to my longing.
Much I learned in the shade of your presence
and more I've become since.
Fly you must.
None loved you greater—
or cared so deep.

In 2014, Shona was again diagnosed with cancer. This time it was located in her rectum. As when she had breast cancer, she was determined to cure herself energetically. She struggled for four years, refusing any sort of conventional treatment, but there came a time when she was forced to seek medical help.

Shona was living at the foot of a mountain in Crozet, Virginia in 2019 when her doctors at the University of Virginia Medical School discovered and removed a massive tumor. That year, Serena and Adin moved her to an apartment in Charlottesville, Virginia to be closer to her care. In the process, she sold her beloved grand piano and lost contact with her many friends around Crozet.

Jay & Shona | November 2014

Shona & Jay at Serena's Wedding | October 2018
Our Last Photograph Together
© Jason Collins

Shortly afterwards, on February 11, 2019, Shona entered Hospice House, The Hospice of the Piedmont, in Charlottesville, never to leave. This was the beginning of the end of another one of Shona's many lives across time.

The hospice was an old Victorian home across from the First Presbyterian Church of Charlottesville that held six or eight patients. The nurses there were incredible beings of light. They allowed Shona to decorate her room as if it were her home, complete with candles and her artwork. The conditions could not have been better for the woman I loved.

I traveled to be with Shona on February 11th and a remarkable thing happened. A harpist entered her room and begins playing angelic music. It was a portable harp, only eight pounds. Shona asked to play and the harp was carefully laid on Shona's chest. Shona has not played a harp since age 18, yet all the music and the fingering came back to her instantly. Shona played flawlessly and I was moved beyond beauty as a witness to this extraordinary moment.

I came again to her on February 25th to stay. With Serena's approval, they gave Shona liquid morphine to ease her pain. I never knew if she wanted that and I felt even more helpless. Since we were divorced, I no longer had any say as her next of kin.

What was it like to be with my beloved Shona at the end? She had been unconscious for some time, unable to speak, so no one knew her final words, but she was able to hear to the last. I sing to her, I read to her, I tell her funny things to make her laugh inside, with Serena stoically watching.

I hold the energy for her without weeping. I am by her side two days later at 1:38 pm when the young nurse takes her pulse, then says, "She is gone."

Shona flies away in peace, effortlessly, on her own terms. The tears and pain are somehow surmountable, her last gift to me. I would do it all again willingly. I begin to yell, "darling, my darling," over and over. The tears come and Serena puts her arm around me in silence.

We leave about 30 minutes later as the hospice took over the process. I never saw the love of my life again. But I knew that all was well. Her words rang in my heart, "All is well."

Death and grief are such intimate truths. I confess that Shona's threw me back into the painful past of reliving Carolyn's slow death.

When Carolyn died, I was so overcome that I could not even give her eulogy. Until I met Shona, I did not understand why I could not finish my grieving for Carolyn, but 30 years later Shona guided me to complete that healing—one of the many gifts Shona showered upon me.

Shona was cremated on March 20, 2019 in Richmond, Virginia. Serena organized *Shona: A Celebration of Her Life* held at the Unity Church of Charlottesville on May 11, 2019. My good friend Chuck Eisenberg was there to support me. Fred had told me at Serena's wedding that this was his farewell to his Mum—he would not be returning from Los Angeles when she died. Adin, for his own reasons, did not attend. Ben and family were there, but Camilla had graduate school classes she could not miss.

There were about 100 people there. Together, we offered this prayer for her:

> *Great Mother-Father Spirit, our source, ground of our being, and giver of meaning—This is our prayer in celebration of the wonderful life of Shona Bellew.*
>
> *We rejoice in the life and light you gave to Shona and the gifts she gave back even more to us and this world.*
>
> *Shona continually reminded us of the power of courage to restore happiness and hope, to forgive what once was, and to choose again. She became what you created her to be, a reminder again and again that love of self and others is our only true reality on earth, the power within that makes us all part of one humanity, and our connection to the divine.*

Today, we also celebrate Shona. We will keep loving her as
she loved us. She taught us to grow and understand, to be wise
and strong, kind and good, and unafraid.
    Shona was a miracle, and a blessing to us all. Shona smiled
on us and brought a new light to our souls. She came here and
made the world better and more beautiful.
    This is our prayer for Shona.
    And all is well. Amen.

Kate Tamakin Arnold played the harp as her gift to Shona. She originated the clinical program Music by the Bedside for Hospice of the Piedmont. Kate is also music director laureate of the Charlottesville Symphony at the University of Virginia.

Serena spoke and I was able to share my eulogy for Shona with those who had come to celebrate her:

Forever will I remember you
and forever will I know
the parts of me now with you,
you the best of this man's dreams:
woman-flower, child-laugher,
kiss-blower, touch-healer,
peace bringing, high dreaming,
head helping, heart mending you.

As best I remember, Shona's dear friends, Mira and Anne-Marie, spoke with tears flowing.

After the service, my granddaughter, Ellery, walked up to Kate interested in her harp. Kate took the time to let her try. She said that Ellery was a natural with fingering and ambidextrous with both hands, a rare but crucial harp skill. High tea was served at the reception, accompanied by a rolling show of photographs across Shona's entire life. We served her favorite, Lapsang Souchong, and mine, Golden Monkey.

On September 20th, Serena flew to England to scatter her ashes at Castlerigg Stone Circle, the very place Shona and I had visited, and where Shona may have once danced as a Druid.

Shona's Ashes | September 19, 2019
© Serena Bellew Welshans

Eulogy for Shona
April 4, 1941 – February 27, 2019
(11 May 2019)

Shona was the love and light of my life and I was her champion. She set me on fire so I now am a light of my own. She showered kindness upon me and loved me beyond belief. Shona was my best friend, trusted confidant, spiritual counselor, mentor, artistic inspiration, editor, and greatest fan, fellow adventurer and world traveler, wife, and soul partner. Shona was also a great teacher.

I didn't know the truth of who I was until I met Shona 22 years ago. She brought a new and better kind of joy to my life.

Early on, I wrote this song for her:

We met one long September day;
I was so scared you heard me say.
You judged me not, just touched my heart,

and time made clear we'd never part.
We were so young within our hearts,
for there we found our sacred parts.

We filled our cup to overflow
and sent out love to all we know.

I ask you dear, will you be mine, as we share this slice of time?
For we are bound by destiny to love and laugh, and simply be.

So, let me say I love you so and watch your face begin to glow,
And hear you talk about our life:
the dreams we have as man and wife.

One life I want to spend with you, adventure as the way we do.
I'll treasure you, as you will me; our honest days will keep us free.

Earth has lost one of its gifted participants, one who explored and knew and taught the patterns of life and beauty and how they made meaning of our existence. Shona was the wisest and bravest woman I have ever known, and the most beautiful spiritual goddess, inside and out, I have ever known, too.

She taught me a path to my own happiness, to my internal place of peace.

I wrote this to her:

You don't care that I'm weak,
you don't judge if I cry,
you're not afraid when I lose control,
but you see how I try.
You let me mourn each loss.
You forgive what I said.
You smile when I screw up the tickets
and when we love in bed.
You help the releasing
of malfunctions in me
by blessing me each murky moment,
stumbling to get free.
My life is not pretty

when I live in my cave,
but I really believe when you tell me
I'm your man and you think I am brave.

To me she was a bright, bubbling soul who could not be captured and kept in a bottle. I wrote about that this way:

I never really had you;
I just enjoyed your presence,
a glow in time
across a wonderful sea,
something I will
never lose or leave:
something about you
that became
something more
about me.
Ah, what we said,
what we did,
what we were,
when we were together.

She was an elegant beauty and playful as a child at the same time. Her voice soothed me; her ideas taught me; her words inspired me, her smile dared me; her energy infected me; and her heart opened mine. And I loved her for all that. She glowed like a soft, insistent beacon, living an adventure of sharing herself with anyone of similar daring. She had about her a childlike whimsy and an elegant femininity decorated with laughter, altogether a stunning soul. She challenged me and I grew.

I simply enjoyed her vibrant living. She added great value to this world. She forgave all the many who had wronged her and had not an enemy in the world.

I once gave her a gold ring inscribed on the outside with *Shona was created to be treasured.* And she once inscribed my bracelet with these words, *Jay is an innocent man.* On the back of it, I added what she said to me, *And Shona adores him.*

Shona played the harp, the piano, the organ, she danced and drummed in the Olympic Games, she survived a very abusive childhood and a murdered child. She was a British officer's daughter,

146

a debutante, aristocrat, and socialite, a prolific spiritual artist, bit actress, sportswear model, published author and poet, management consultant, public speaker, workshop and seminar presenter, an ordained minister, a counselor who helped many lives besides mine and spread her wisdom and joy far across this planet she loved.

She was an innovative educator and school founder. She was a ski instructor, Junior Wimbledon tennis player, catcher on an adult men's baseball team, an experienced hot air balloon pilot on both sides of the Atlantic who survived a crash and fire, teacher, innovative educator, school founder, and fund raiser, Formula 2 racing mechanic, bricklayer, student of many religions, an intuitive healer, yoga and meditation practitioner, professional travel guide, published poet and author, a breast cancer survivor on her own terms, airline hostage survivor, voiceover narrator, and ethereal choral vocalist.

Shona was an environmentalist; she had that marvelous sense of wonder for the natural world and she re-infected me with it. She lived in over 50 permanent places on four continents and took me to visit the world, fluent in three languages. In short, Shona was my hero and the most honest human I have ever known. Her presence left a permanent improvement on this planet. And I could make her laugh. That sound to my ears was a delight like no other, and I called her Giggles.

She helped me save my own life more than once from my own traumas of childhood and combat. She knew the depth of my day. She helped mentor my children's lives and my grandchildren, too.

One thing I did for Shona was introduce her to Mark Twain, my favorite author in the world. Shona couldn't understand him as I did until I started reading his words to her with the energy and drawl of my Southern rebel boy. Then he became a shared delight the same way I introduced her to *Calvin and Hobbes*. She always wanted me to perform in character as Mark Twain on stage, and even gave me a wig and fake moustache. What a compliment and belief in me that was.

She was the biggest believer in my writing. Since I met her, she caused me to write hundreds of thousands of words. She did the same for the many thousands of my photographs. Because of her, I got published, won awards, and have two book covers to my credit.

Her loyalty and trust in me and my talent was unconditional. Real men faithfully love such rare, real women.

Shona was a powerful, multi-talented modern renaissance woman. Her life was purposed here. She possessed a great dignity of spirit, one of the many things I secretly adored about her. If you believe in a higher power, whatever the name, some unknowable mystery greater than ourselves, then you understood, in part, the heart of Shona. With each other, Shona and I could be our real selves, revealing every fear and dream. And we could be our magical kids.

She left behind the gifts of her beautiful children. She told me the children she raised were never a trouble to her. She wanted them and she let them be their adventurous selves. I am happy to have such wonderful relationships with all of them. Serena, Fred, and Adin, and their spouses, are a warm part of my extended family.

Shona was not silent, she spoke up and took a stand; she was unconquered and unconquerable. So I wrote this song about her:

> *Wild women don't get the blues.*
> *They shake out their hair and take off their shoes.*
> *They laugh and they love with nothing to lose.*
> *Wonderful, wild women don't get the blues.*
>
> *Wild women never are slow.*
> *They beat you to bed and don't treat you low.*
> *They sparkle in rain, they let children grow.*
> *Wonderful wild women, blues they don't know.*
>
> *Heaven is full of wild women from here,*
> *Singing and playing with nothing to fear,*
> *Sending us music that's sensual, clear,*
> *And telling each man, hold your wild woman dear.*
>
> *Wild women don't get the blues.*
> *Wild women just can't get the blues.*

Shona was the best friend I ever had or anyone could ever want. She was my emotional revelator. I trusted her and no one else with my life, even with the lives of my children and my grandchildren.

I would die in battle for her, but more important I would live for her, and, most important of all, I will live for me as she showed me by example.

Shona taught me a truth I never knew before, that love shines on the shadows to be healed, so I learned to welcome the shadows as the gifts they are. We used that and our love to heal our wounds.

I will be fully happy and I will keep pursuing my dreams in honor of our life here together, in honor of you, Shona, and in honor of me, your most challenging and most determined pupil, and your biggest fan.

I have fought in war and have never seen such great moral, physical, emotional, creative, and spiritual courage as I saw in her. The loss of her to me, to you, and to the world she made tangibly better cannot be replaced, and that is why I grieve so much for the wonder of life she shared with me.

The professional warrior in me would like nothing better than to go back in time and hold all those people accountable for their wrong deeds against this innocent child and innocent woman, but I came to learn from Shona a better lesson from her own spiritual heart that she also saw hidden in mine. She taught me that awakeness, awareness, and acceptance of self is a greater freedom than merely forgiving others.

She remained the brightest lovelight I have ever seen. Hers was a great soul, and ours was the greatest love we ever knew. I have written tens of thousands of words in prose and verse to record some of her story, her incredible wisdom, and our love, perhaps difficult for many to believe, but still true.

My words today are one way I celebrate and honor her remarkable life. I wrote this for her:

I tell you grand ideas;
you encourage with sparkled eyes.
Then I melt in you.

I build great structures in my mind,
heroic tasks, wonderful victories.
Then I melt in you.

I wax on about the meaning of history
and wonder out loud if I am in it.
Then I melt in you.

I utter serious things;
you find the humor inside.
Then I melt in you.

I puff my feathers into a splendid man;
you remind me of my pure truth.
Then I melt in you.

I think I know you,
but better you know me,
distilling my heart with your relentless love.

I can tell you anything,
and you cannot restrain
from blessing my unguarded soul.

And then I melt in you.

Shona was a unique beacon of possibilities guiding me in many ways. She had the power to carry her own weather. She made her own sunshine, gentle rain, and clean breezes wherever she was, and whenever she wanted it. I watched her do this all the time.

We also shared an absolute trust without betrayal, without judgment, based on full, honest disclosure. We never made each other wrong. That's a remarkable thing for two lovers like us to say who were betrayed so often so young by close adult authority in charge of our care.

We shared everything, all our dreams, all our shadows, never withholding anything. She knew me better than I knew myself and explained my dark deeds of war to me so I could create compassion for myself and then others. I am a blessed and better man because she entered my life. The day I met Shona the entire universe redirected me toward my destiny, a lost wanderer no more. If miracles do exist, our meeting was mine.

Since before I met her, she has been guided by the universe to create spiritual artwork. She did her art for its own sake, not hers.

She had to, for that was her calling. None of that art was her creation; she was merely the vehicle for recording it in visible form. In her art, she sought great truth beneath the chaos. These tangible gifts she leaves to the world as part of her legacy.

I want the world to know that Shona and I had a wonderful, magical life together, married and apart. And I would do it all over again, every bit of it, in a St. Louis second. I never lived so rich, so fully alive, as I did with her presence in my life.

Before she got sick, I wrote this poem:

If I am to lose you, pray thee it be a lovely day,
as you have always shone and been to me,
sparkles of sun mid a gentle rain.

If I could, I would hold you forever in safe arms
and tell you again of your own treasure
ringed in gold that I fell into happily and safely
as a bird gliding home.

Shona: ah, what a woman; what a love; what a life we shared that passed too quickly, now to last forever in my memory.

I'll be seeing you there, darling, where everyone is kind and loving, to laugh and play in the fields of the divine, you and I finally safely home. Tonight, I'll meet you in my dreams where the river meets the sea.

Shona | June 2010

Dénouement

As I said at the beginning, I intended to tell my truth. I must also say here that I never intended in this work to hurt any other living soul, or myself, or Shona most of all. If your truth disagrees with mine, I encourage you to write yours down as I did.

I treasure my relationships with family and friends. Relationships bind the world together. By another name, it is community, and community heals its members.

In completing this biography of Shona's life, one thing is obvious to me about her. As a child, Shona stayed alive without any peer or adult mentor interested in her well-being. She had no example to follow, no one to encourage her, no one to confide in, no one to seek advice. She was emotionally naked, vulnerable, and alone.

I don't see how any child in her circumstance could have endured as she did, unconquered. But she did, anyway. Shona turned within and found her inner spirit there. That inner spirit became her needed mentor, both consciously and unconsciously. She then found ways to heal herself and many, many others.

I see Shona's life as an example of what is possible in impossible situations.

It is my prayer, and I know it was hers, that other children and grownups will discover their spiritual nature and not only survive, but prevail. It is my wish that sharing her story will inspire others to do so, bringing a gift of hope to humanity.

Darling Shona, how many ways can I say I love you? This heart knows. And I was happiest when I made you laugh. And so it is. And all is well.

Acknowledgments

The birth of this book baby needed help. It took the skilled support of a literary midwife, Karen Mireau, founder of Azalea Art Press in California. Without her care and talent this book would still be a dream. She has my highest praise and recommendation.

And her co-conspirator is my friend, Elizabeth Perlman, who nudged me with the idea of telling Shona's story in April of 2020. I think Elizabeth was Shona's greatest fan, besides me. She connected me to Karen Mireau. Both women understood Shona as a soul sister. They cajoled and guided me as I think Shona would have wanted. May these ladies thrive on.

My family supported me all the way: my children, Camilla and Ben, and the grandkids, River, Maia, Journey, Luke, and Ellery. All of them were loved by Shona; and they loved Shona, and still do.

My friends Christine Erwin and Carla McDonald helped with important research.

I want to mention the budding photographers in my family: granddaughters, Journey Carolyn Collins and her sister, Maia Carolyn.

I want to thank the contributors who took the time to tell their personal stories about Shona: Camilla Collins, Alain de Cadenet, Chuck Eisenberg, Laura Chason Love, and Sherry Wheat.

Paul Wiehagen, staff engineer at Shock City Studios in St. Louis, Missouri did a wonderful job recording and editing my reading of the book for *audible.com*. Gratefully, only he and I know my slurs, mispronunciations, and stray noises that you will never have to hear.

Shona's daughter, Serena, gifted me with all of Shona's original paintings (that I have yet to finish counting for an inventory and catalog), and other personal possessions of Shona. I was honored when Serena asked me to read a passage from *The Velveteen Rabbit* at her wedding to Cory Welshans as Shona listened. Thank you, Serena.

I am especially grateful to Mark Waterhouse of Happy Jack Graphics in Clayton, Georgia, who returned one-of-a-kind scanned files of some of Shona's art that would have otherwise been lost forever. Now prints of her drawings can go out into the world as she wanted.

Of crucial importance to this book was the work of all the extremely compassionate and competent nurses, staff, and support persons associated with Hospice of the Piedmont in Charlottesville, Virginia. But one example is they let Shona decorate her room as if she were at home. Love permeated the air there. If I were a truly wealthy man, I would clone Hospice of the Piedmont across this country such is their quality of care.

This book took me to and through elation and despair repeatedly, but, all in all, it was a worthy memory journey and my labor of love.

Print Book | EBook Orders
The book formats above are available from:
Lulu.com, Amazon.com, BarnesandNoble.com

Audio Book Orders
Audio Books can be ordered directly from:
Audible.com

Signed Editions
To receive a signed edition of this book:
please email Jay Harden at gjphotography2020@gmail.com
with your mailing address and how you wish it inscribed.
Your payment of $25, which includes shipping,
can be made via PayPal at jay@jayharden.com.
Credit cards are also welcomed at PayPal.

Art Prints
Reproductions of Shona's art may be ordered directly from the
Etsy shop **SpiritOnFire**. The high resolution 13" x 19" color prints
will be mailed to you for $65 each, which includes shipping.

Poetry | Photo | Art
Credits
All photographs © Jay Harden unless noted in the text.

Chapter heading poetry excerpts © Jay Harden.

Cover design by Elizabeth Perlman
elizabeth@intuitivewritingproject.org

Page iii
Shona Harden 11" x 14" egg tempera watercolor on birch wood
based on photograph of Shona by Jay Harden September 22, 2001

Nonprofit Charity Donations

All net profits from **Spirit on Fire**
will go to Shona's favorite charities:

La Leche League International
https://www.llli.org

Tiggywinkles Wildlife Hospital
https://www.sttiggywinkles.org.uk

and National Audubon Society
https://www.audubon.org

Author Jay Harden
© Journey Carolyn Collins

About the Author

Jay Harden grew up in Georgia envying the eagles and hawks, ditching his shoes in summer, and adventuring the alleys, trees, and creeks. Since the beginning, his life has been defined by moments of truth, planned and unplanned.

He survived air combat in Vietnam and navigated his B-52 crew safely home 63 times. After active duty he served in the Missouri Air National Guard and pursued a science career in the Department of Defense, retiring in 1997.

While at the DoD, he helped develop the world's first digital mapping system and co-authored a ground-breaking technical handbook on cartography that was widely distributed in the Defense Department and beyond. He has since published in numerous anthologies and privately published multiple volumes of family history, poetry, and journals.

It was a twist of fate that led Jay to meeting Shona, the woman who would irrevocably alter his life. Together they explored a completely new universe, delving into esoteric realms Jay had never before imagined and finding an enduring love.

Thanks to Shona's encouragement, Jay lived in India for an extended time studying yoga, completed a sacred warrior weekend, and deepened his passion for poetry, songwriting, and photography.

This tribute to Shona, his soulmate and mentor, fulfills his promise to her to share her extraordinary, inspiring story with the world. He now spends his days writing, photographing, playing guitar, and learning from his five amazing grandchildren.

To Contact the Author:
gjphotography2020@gmail.com
https://spiritonfire2020.blogspot.com

To Contact the Publisher:
Azalea.Art.Press@gmail.com
https://azaleaartpress.blogspot.com

Made in the USA
Middletown, DE
09 December 2020

27114679R00099